# CRICKET
# WORLD CUP
# 2007 GUIDE

# CRICKET WORLD CUP 2007 GUIDE

## THE INDEPENDENT GUIDE TO THE WORLD CHAMPIONSHIP OF ONE-DAY CRICKET

CHRIS HAWKES

CARLTON

First published by Carlton Books 2007
Copyright © Carlton Books Limited 2007

The publisher has taken reasonable steps to check the
accuracy of the facts contained herein at the time of going
to press, but can take no responsibility for any errors.

A CIP catalogue record of this book is available upon
request.

ISBN 10: 1-84442-084-1
ISBN 13: 978-1-84442-084-1

Commissioning Editor: Martin Corteel
Assistant Editor: David Ballheimer
Project Art Editor: Luke Griffin
Designer: David Etherington
Picture Research: Paul Langan
Production: Lisa French

Printed and bound in Dubai

Carlton Books

**Publisher's notes**
All statistics correct to the end of the ICC Champions
Trophy Final, 5 November 2006
All start times are 9.30 am local time.

This book has been prepared without any involvement on
the part of the International Cricket Council or any related
bodies. Carlton Books is not affiliated or associated with
the International Cricket Council in any way.

## ABOUT THE AUTHOR

CHRIS HAWKES, a former youth international and first-
class cricketer with Leicestershire CCC (1990–92), is an
experienced writer and editor, specializing in sport, who
has worked on numerous titles for an array of publishers
on an assortment of subjects. He lives in London.

**Title page:** Caribbean sports fans love their cricket.
**Page 2 (clockwise from top left):** West Indies fans
celebrate a special moment at Port of Spain, Trinidad;
Skipper Ricky Ponting of Australia is chaired off the ground
after leading his team to win the 2003 World Cup Final;
A fan waits for the rain to stop during the Sri Lanka v.
South Africa match at Durban in the 2003 World Cup; The
Paksiton team celebrate after winning the 1992 World Cup
Final at Melbourne; India shocked the cricketing world by
defeating the West Indies in the 1983 World Cup Final.
**Right:** West Indies all-rounder Dwayne Bravo is greeted
by some young fans in in his native Trinidad.

# CONTENTS

# INTRODUCTION

**Every sport has its pinnacle: athletes train day and night to compete in the Olympic Games; footballers hone their skills on the training pitch dreaming of World Cup glory; cyclists pound the endless alpine slopes to prepare themselves for the Tour de France; and rugby players pump weights and knock down tackle bag after tackle bag to secure their place in a team with a shot at their game's greatest prize. And cricketers are no different.**

A tournament like the Cricket World Cup adds reason to early-morning runs, it breaks the monotony of the gym sessions and encourages the extra hours spent in the nets perfecting reverse-swing bowling or honing the on-drive.

It's a tournament that creates dreams: children from as far apart as Mumbai, Melbourne and Manchester will sneak out of the house to continue their version of cricket's greatest competition, all hoping to clip the winning runs through the leg side or to be the bowler who sends the middle stump cart-wheeling out of the ground to bring their side World Cup glory. Who knows who this tournament will inspire among the Test cricketers of tomorrow.

It may not have been universally welcomed when it was first staged in 1975 – indeed, England were the only country who would agree to host the tournament – but the Cricket World Cup has been a spectacular success; it is the only cricket tournament that will grab such a huge global audience – an estimated 2.2 billion people will tune in to the 2007 incarnation of the competition. And cricket is unique in another sense: it is one of the few sports where fans from different cultures, continents and religions will unite behind a single cause – to see their country crowned as the champions of the world.

The ninth edition of the Cricket World Cup could not have chosen a more spectacular location. The West Indies is the only one of the original six Test-playing nations never to have hosted a World Cup. How could a team playing under the united banner of so many different countries stage one of the largest sporting events in the world, the critics argued.

Time has eased such logistical concerns. Travelling today is as straightforward and as cost-effective as it has ever been, and spectators will travel to the Caribbean in their thousands. New grounds have been built and old grounds – some of which date back to 1928 – have been updated to provide both a state-of-the-art spectator experience and a cricket legacy in the Caribbean that will extend long after the moment the final ball has been bowled.

But this tournament will be as much about the experiences on offer beyond the boundary rope as it will be about the cut-and-thrust action on the field of play. The Caribbean has long been established as a tourist Mecca. The tournament itself has wisely been sold to prospective punters as a tourist experience of a lifetime as much as a cricket experience.

You can lie on spectacular white-sand beaches, trek through rainforests, peer inside the crater of an active volcano, bask in the spray of some of the world's most spectacular waterfalls and dive among the world's most abundant reefs before sampling the delights of Caribbean cuisine and washing it all down with an iced cocktail based on the omnipresent rum.

The West Indies is one of cricket's many spiritual homes. Don't be surprised to find the streets of Kingston, Port of Spain and Bridgetown deserted the moment the nation's heroes take to the field of play. Expect to savour the carnival atmosphere inside the grounds: the steel drums will ring through the stands and the locals will be sure to offer their considered opinion on the state of the game.

It is set to be a tournament that will live long in the memory ... for players and spectators alike.

**Location, location, location:** It may have taken some time for the Cricket World Cup to reach the Caribbean, but cricket fans will be in for a treat, both during and after the hours of play.

# ABOUT THE CRICKET WORLD CUP

**Since 1930 and every four years thereafter – bar a break for the Second World War – football fans have looked forward to the World Cup. It seems strange, given that cricket's rules and regulations predate football's by one hundred years, that it took cricket's authorities so long to organize a similar event.**

## ORIGINS OF THE CRICKET WORLD CUP

It wasn't through want of trying. The first attempt to stage any kind of world championship came in 1912, when a three-way series was arranged between the then Test-playing nations: England, Australia and South Africa. It was a disaster, ruined primarily by the weather, and any thoughts of repeating the idea were dropped.

It wasn't until 1975, on the back of the rising popularity of the one-day game, that the six Test-playing nations of the time – Australia, England, India, New Zealand, Pakistan and the West Indies – were joined by Sri Lanka and East Africa in the first ever World Cup.

It may not have been to the purists' liking when it kicked off, but the tournament has been an outstanding success. A global audience of 2.2 billion in over 200 countries is estimated to tune in to the 51 matches that will make up the 2007 edition of the Cricket World Cup.

## CARIBBEAN CHALLENGE

And the event itself will be unique. Whatever the result, the West Indies will have achieved what no other sporting event has ever achieved before: it will have staged a world sporting event across nine countries, all of which are separated by water.

It is vital that the West Indian cricket authorities get it right. Cricket in the Caribbean, already in the doldrums, will be in grave danger without the money from the Cricket World Cup; in recent years, financial problems have beset the national team. But, as the opening ceremony

drew ever nearer, the indications were that the cricket authorities, with the help of the local governments, had things firmly under control. It has certainly been a team effort.

The challenge has not only been to make sure that the stadiums are ready; it has been to make sure that the host venues themselves will be ready. The massive influx of tourists (100,000 unique tourists – people travelling solely to the region to watch the tournament – in addition to the normal influx of tourists to the region) will provide a huge boost to the region's economy – it is easy to forget that the Caribbean is a far from prosperous region. On average, each tourist will spend US$200 per day on accommodation, travel, food, entertainment and souvenirs. A successfully organized tournament will go a long way to enhancing an already vibrant tourist industry that is so necessary to the Caribbean.

## TICKETS

Over 800,000 tickets have been made available for cricket fans. They will be able to choose between the cheapest single-match tickets and the US$2,000-per-person-and-rising suite package (for six people), which gives full accreditation for a suite for each of the group games at a ground. Fans should note that tickets for group matches involving the West Indies, England, Australia and India are more expensive. To enhance the tourist experience, each team will be based on one island for the group stages: for example, England are in St Lucia, Australia and South Africa are in St Kitts, India are in Trinidad and Pakistan are in Jamaica for the duration of the group stages.

## PRIME LOCATION

Of course, the Caribbean is the perfect location for the ninth Cricket World Cup. It has been pitched to prospective spectators as much as a tourist experience as it has been touted as a cricket experience; for those who travel, it is sure to be the experience of a lifetime.

The tourist infrastructure in the area is already well established; one of the major questions when the West Indies were invited to host the tournament for the first time, was how would the stadiums stand up to the influx of 16 international teams (the largest of any Cricket World Cup) and their travelling support?

## A LASTING LEGACY

Major global sporting events are as much about the legacy left in the host nation as they are about the sporting action that takes place on the field of play. By the time the Cricket World Cup circus packs its big top and heads out of town, the West Indies will have state-of-the-art cricket facilities.

Five new stadiums have been constructed, existing grounds – some of which date back to 1928 – have been upgraded to the tune of US$250 million, a figure that is set to double when expenditure on technology has been taken into account.

Before a ball has been bowled, the 2007 Cricket World Cup will have provided a major, and much-needed, boost to cricket in the Caribbean. In an ideal world, the West Indies, the sleeping giants of world cricket, will raise their weary heads and, come the end of the tournament, walk off with the greatest prize in the game.

# THE RULES AND REGULATIONS

## TOURNAMENT FORMAT

Sixteen teams will contest the 2007 Cricket World Cup: the 11 nations with one-day international status, plus the five qualifiers from the 2005 ICC Trophy in Ireland.

### Group Stage

There will be four groups of four teams, with ache side playing each other once. Two points are awarded for a win, one for a tie or a no result, and none for a loss. The top two teams from each group will progress to the Super Eight stage. In the event of two sides finishing level on points, the team with the higher run-rate will progress. If the two teams still cannot be separated, the team with the higher number of wickets taken per balls bowled will progress. In the unlikely event they still cannot be separated, lots will be drawn.

### Super Eight

Each team will play every other qualified team except for the team it played in the group stage. The top four teams will progress to the semi-finals. If two teams finish level on points, the higher-placed team will be decided in the following way:

- most wins throughout the competition against the other Super Eight qualifiers.
- if still equal, the team with the highest net run-rate against all Super Eight qualifiers.
- if still equal, the team with the higher number of wickets taken per balls balled.
- if still equal, lots will be drawn.

### Semi-finals

The top-placed team from the Super Eight will play the fourth-placed team and the second-placed the third. In the event of a tie, teams shall compete in a bowl-out to determine the winner. In the event of a no result, the team with the highest run-rate in the Super Eight will progress to the final. If still equal, lots will be drawn.

### Final

In the event of a tied match, there will be a bowl-out to determine the winner. In the event of a no result, the teams will be declared joint winners.

## CONDITIONS OF PLAY

- 50 overs per side: to constitute a match, a minimum of 20 overs need to be received by the team batting second.
- Ten-over limit for bowlers.
- One bouncer per over (i.e. above shoulder height of an upright stance).
- Hours of play:

| | |
|---|---|
| First session: | 0930–1300 |
| Interval: | 1300–1345 |
| Second session: | 1345–1715 |

### Fielding Restrictions

There will be 20 overs of fielding restrictions per side. The first ten overs must come in the first ten overs of the innings. The remaining ten overs will be taken at the discretion of the fielding captain in two blocks of five at any time after that. If they do not choose to exercise this discretion, the overs will commence at the latest available point in the innings (i.e. the 41st over or the 46th). If the game is shortened, the number of fielding restriction overs are altered accordingly.

During fielding restriction overs the following rules will apply:
- only two fielders are allowed beyond a 30-yard (27.43-metre) restriction zone.

During the first ten overs only, in addition to normal fielding restriction over rules:
- two fielders must be stationary in the 15-yard (13.72-metre) zone.

At all times, the following restrictions apply:
- at instant of delivery there may be no more than five fielders on the leg side.
- no more than five fielders are allowed beyond the 30-yard zone.

## HOWZAT!

For the armchair fan, the language of cricket can be quite baffling – if not to say highly amusing. Here is a beginner's guide to some of the more obscure terminology that might emanate from the commentary box during the tournament.

**Beamer:** A fast, head-high delivery that fails to bounce, which the umpire will normally deem a no-ball.

**Bouncer:** A delivery that is short and fast, and fires up towards the batsman's head. If the ball bounces too high (i.e. above shoulder height), then the umpire will call a wide.

**Duck:** When a batsman is given out without scoring a run.

**Fine leg:** A fielder who stands on the leg side of the wicket, but behind where the batsman stands in relation to the wicket.

**Golden duck:** Term used for the score of nought when a batsman has been given out on his first ball without scoring a run.

**Googly:** An off-break delivery by the bowler to a right-handed batsman which is delivered with a leg-break action to deceive the batsman.

**Grubber:** A delivery by the bowler that rolls along the ground.

**Hawkeye:** Technology used by television companies to track the course of the ball after leaving the bowler's hand; particularly helpful for determining lbw decisions.

**Leg side:** The side of the field where the batsman stands when batting; with a right-hand batsman, it is the right side of the field looking down the pitch at him.

**Maiden:** An over in which no runs have been scored.

**Popping crease:** This runs 4ft in front of and parallel to each wicket. The batsman must stand within this area, or he can be given out by the umpire. If any part of his body or his bat is behind the line, then he cannot be given out.

**Reverse sweep:** A mirror image of the sweep shot but where the batsman tries to hit the ball through the off side with a horizontal bat.

**Round the wicket:** An approach whereby the bowler delivers the ball from the hand further from the stumps.

**Runner:** A player who runs between the wickets for a batsman who is unable to take the run himself due to injury.

**Shooter:** A fast delivery by the bowler which stays low.

**Silly point:** A fielder who stands very close to the wicket on the off side, slightly forward of square.

**Sticky wicket:** A damp surface that leads to the ball bouncing erratically. The batsman usually finds it extremely difficult to hit the ball as a result.

**Sweep:** A shot taken by the batsman in which he helps the ball on its way, rather than fiercely striking it. The batsman will bend his right leg to drop his body close to the ground and then swing the bat round to play the ball behind square on the leg side, where the fielding team is allowed to place only two fielders.

**Wicket maiden:** An over in which neither any runs have been scored by a batsman nor a no-ball or wide delivered by the bowler, but a wicket has been taken.

**Yorker:** A delivery from a bowler with the aim of hitting the very bottom of the stumps or bouncing inches in front of them. This is probably the most difficult delivery for a batsman to play an attacking stroke.

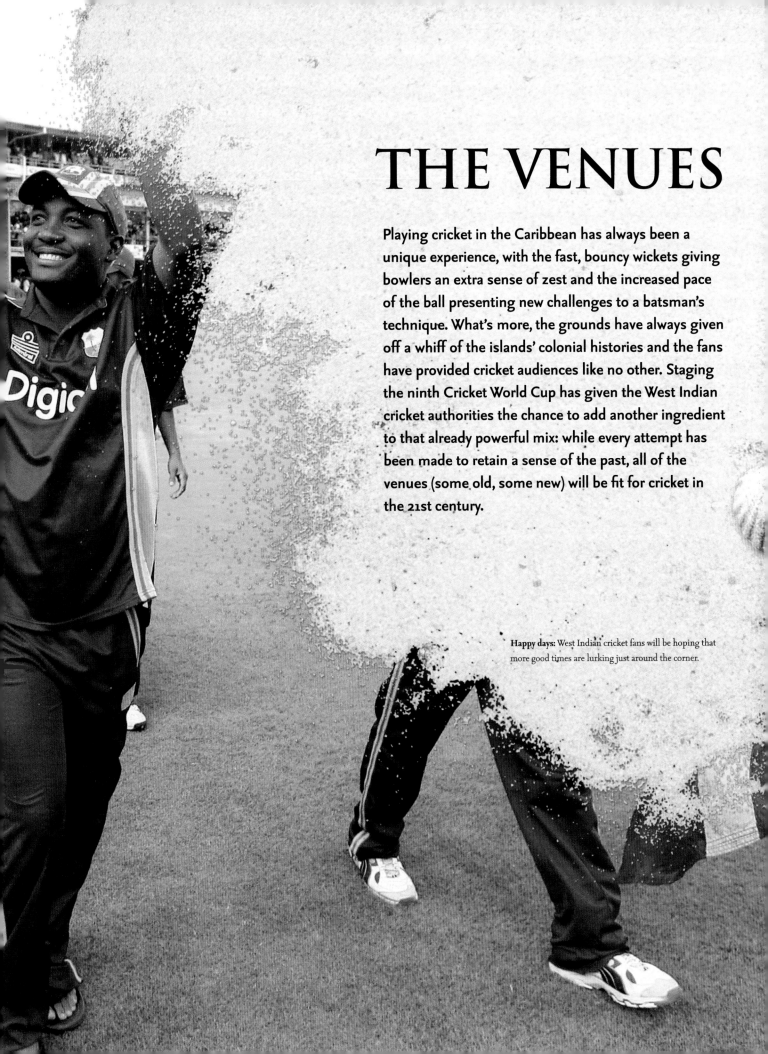

# THE VENUES

Playing cricket in the Caribbean has always been a unique experience, with the fast, bouncy wickets giving bowlers an extra sense of zest and the increased pace of the ball presenting new challenges to a batsman's technique. What's more, the grounds have always given off a whiff of the islands' colonial histories and the fans have provided cricket audiences like no other. Staging the ninth Cricket World Cup has given the West Indian cricket authorities the chance to add another ingredient to that already powerful mix: while every attempt has been made to retain a sense of the past, all of the venues (some old, some new) will be fit for cricket in the 21st century.

**Happy days:** West Indian cricket fans will be hoping that more good times are lurking just around the corner.

# THE GROUNDS

Following the announcement that the West Indies would play host to the 2007 World Cup, plans were put in place to ensure that the tournament would leave a lasting legacy around the islands. Outside money, in the form of loans and grants, was sought, and money poured in from around the world, particularly from China, India and Taiwan.

The money was much-needed. While lying comfortably on a sun-lounger sipping your cocktail on the palm-shaded, white-sanded private beach of a luxury, all-inclusive hotel, it is all too easy to forget that the West Indies is anything but a prosperous region; all too many people there live on or under the poverty line. Any investment that came was put to better use than improving cricket grounds.

The announcement that the ninth Cricket World Cup would be staged in the Caribbean provided an opportunity to change that. It gave the West Indian cricket authorities the chance to take a long look at the state of Caribbean cricket – it has been beset by financial problems over recent years – and plan for

the game's future growth (many local youngsters have turned to American sports).

With more than $250 million already spent on building new stadiums and upgrading old, famous grounds, a figure that is expected to double by the time the first ball is bowled, the World Cup will leave an indelible mark on the islands' cricket future.

**RIGHT: A familiar sight:** Cranes and scaffolding have dominated the Caribbean's cricket venues in the build-up to the Cricket World Cup. The results will be impressive.
**OPPOSITE: Blast from the past:** Views such as this, taken from a West Indies v. Australia one-day international in Grenada, will be a thing of the past. Brand-new, state-of-the-art stadiums will provide a new Caribbean cricketing experience.

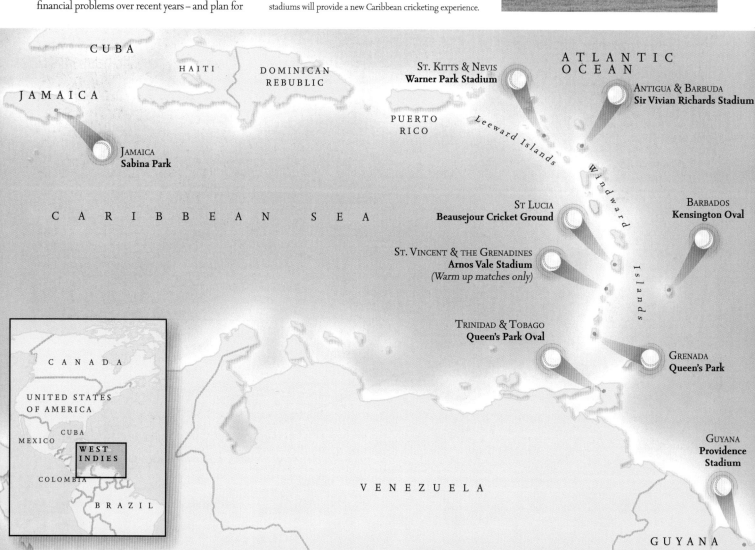

CUBA

JAMAICA

HAITI

DOMINICAN REBUBLIC

ST. KITTS & NEVIS
**Warner Park Stadium**

ATLANTIC OCEAN

ANTIGUA & BARBUDA
**Sir Vivian Richards Stadium**

PUERTO RICO

*Leeward Islands*

JAMAICA
**Sabina Park**

*Windward Islands*

CARIBBEAN SEA

ST LUCIA
**Beausejour Cricket Ground**

BARBADOS
**Kensington Oval**

ST. VINCENT & THE GRENADINES
**Arnos Vale Stadium**
*(Warm up matches only)*

TRINIDAD & TOBAGO
**Queen's Park Oval**

GRENADA
**Queen's Park**

CANADA

UNITED STATES OF AMERICA

CUBA

MEXICO

WEST INDIES

COLOMBIA

BRAZIL

VENEZUELA

GUYANA
**Providence Stadium**

GUYANA

## QUEEN'S PARK OVAL

**Port of Spain, Trinidad & Tobago**
**Group stage**
**Capacity: 25,000**
**Home team: Trinidad & Tobago**

The largest and, with the stunning northern hills providing a magnificent backdrop, the most picturesque ground in the Caribbean, Queen's Park Oval has an atmosphere all of its own and it has played host to Test matches since 1930. It is a ground that evokes bad memories for England fans: their team were bowled out here for 45 in 1994–95.

## WARNER PARK STADIUM

**Basseterre, St Kitts & Nevis**
**Group stage**
**Capacity: 10,000**
**Home team: Leeward Islands**

When the West Indies played India here in a one-day international on 23 May 2006, Warner Park Stadium became the first of the seven new World Cup stadiums to open. The ground's capacity may be small, but the east side of the ground is stadium-free to allow the prevailing easterly wind to have its cooling effect on the ground.

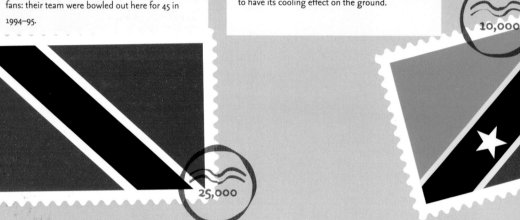

## SIR VIVIAN RICHARDS STADIUM

**St John's, Antigua**
**Super Eights**
**Capacity: 20,000**

Named after the island's most famous player, and built especially for the World Cup, the ground is dominated by two large stands: the north stand, which will house the media, and the southern stand, which incorporates the pavilion and corporate hospitality suites. The grass banks on the east and west side of the ground will provide a magnificent viewing spot.

## QUEEN'S PARK

**St George's, Grenada**
**Super Eights**
**Capacity: 17,000**
**Home team: Windward Islands**

Now home to the West Indies Cricket Academy, Queen's Park – sometimes referred to as the National Cricket Stadium – was one of the first stadiums to benefit from the influx of cash that followed the West Indies' appointment as host nation for the 2007 World Cup. The result is a magnificent 17,000-seater that will play host to Super Eight matches.

## PROVIDENCE STADIUM

**Providence, Guyana**
**Super Eights**
**Capacity: 15,000**

Built at a cost of $30 million, with much of the money – in the form of grants and loans – coming from the Indian government, this state-of-the-art stadium will become Guyana's main ground, superseding the historic ground at Georgetown around seven miles to the north. Grass mounds housing 4,000 spectators will give the stadium that unique Caribbean flavour.

## STAR QUOTE

"The instructions throughout the World Cup were the same – attack." **Imran Khan** shares the secret of Pakistan's 1992 Cricket World Cup success.

## BEAUSEJOUR CRICKET GROUND

**Gros Inlet, St Lucia**
**Group stage and semi-final**
**Capacity: 12,000 (20,000 with temporary seating)**
**Home team: West Indies**

By the time the World Cup circus comes to town, the capacity in this ground will have increased by 8,000 with the inclusion of temporary stands to house 20,000 spectators. Beausejour Cricket Ground is now one of the elder statesmen of Caribbean cricket grounds, despite only having hosted its first one-day international – West Indies v. New Zealand – in 2002.

## SABINA PARK

**Kingston, Jamaica**
**Group stage and semi-final**
**Capacity: 22,000**
**Home team: Jamaica**

A Test venue since 1930 and the recipient of major renovation work prior to the World Cup, Sabina Park was the ground where, in 1958, Garfield Sobers plundered a Test record 365 not out against Pakistan. The fans may have a reputation for being lively and vociferous, but this is a special place to watch cricket.

## KENSINGTON OVAL

**Bridgetown, Barbados**
**Super Eights and Final**
**Capacity: 28,000**
**Home team: Barbados**

The most historic of all the Caribbean grounds, Kensington Oval hosted the first England touring side in 1895; the first combined West Indian side (against the MCC in 1910–11); and was the scene of the West Indies' first Test match, against England in 1930. The ground has been totally rebuilt for the 2007 World Cup and will stage the Final.

## STAR QUOTE

"I think it was one of the finest innings I have seen. He batted so brilliantly, with complete authority. There was no doubt it was a magnificent innings." Sri Lanka's **Hashan Tillakaratne** on Aravinda de Silva's match-winning century in the 1996 World Cup final.

## STAR QUOTE

"That innings was probably a little bit overdue. I have not done much in the lead-up games – but I saved it for the final." **Ricky Ponting** on his World Cup final-winning innings in South Africa in 2003.

# QUALIFYING FOR THE WORLD CUP

**The 2005 ICC Trophy was effectively two competitions within a single tournament. The top two teams from each pool would gain automatic World Cup qualification; the third- and fourth-placed teams would enter a straight knock-out competition for the final World Cup slot.**

When the draw was made, the hosts, Ireland, must have thanked the cricket gods. They had avoided the big guns, who were stacked in group B, and their path to a World Cup debut seemed more straightforward.

They kicked off their campaign in impressive fashion. Ed Joyce smashed a 92-ball 103 to ease them to a 97-run victory over Bermuda. Elsewhere in group A, TM Hansen took 6 for 30 as Denmark beat Uganda and the UAE also got off to a winning start, beating the United States by 55 runs.

Canada and Namibia, both 2003 World Cup participants, squared off in group B's opening rubber. Canada came out on top with a two-run victory. The Netherlands opened with a nine-wicket win over Papua New Guinea, and Scotland strolled to victory against Oman.

Bermuda got back to winning ways in their second-round group A match against the UAE, their 30-run win coming as a surprise to many. Less so Ireland's 127-run victory over Uganda, but the misery continued for the United States when they fell to a 96-run defeat to Denmark.

In group B, fine Scottish bowling restricted Canada to 189 for 8 and the Scots eased to the target with seven overs in hand. Namibia got off the mark with a 96-run win over PNG, but it was the Netherlands who impressed. Anchored by Bas Zuiderent's 119, they amassed 325 for 5. When Oman capitulated to 67 all out, the gulf in class was evident.

Denmark's winning ways came to a halt when they faced Bermuda in their group A third-round clash. The islanders eased to a comfortable 93-run victory. An unbeaten 113 from Ed Joyce saw Ireland to a two-wicket victory over UAE, but it was misery upon misery for the USA as they slipped to a third straight defeat, this time to Uganda.

Scotland's march through group B continued when they ripped through a fragile PNG batting line-up and cantered to the 91 required in 19 overs. John Davison (74) held his nerve to help a stuttering Canada to a two-wicket win over Oman, and the Netherlands notched up a six-wicket victory over Namibia.

Group A's fourth-round matches were washed out meaning the outcome of the group would go down to the wire and the rain had its say in the group B games, but all the matches were completed. Canada hauled themselves to a two-wicket win over the Netherlands. Scotland ensured their World Cup place with a 27-run win over Namibia and PNG recorded a 93-run victory over Oman.

All eyes were on Ireland at Bangor on 7 July 2005; they did not disappoint, ambling to a 73-run victory to leave Denmark in fourth place. Ireland's confirmed debut in the World Cup would have ensured that a few glasses would have been raised on what was an otherwise black day in other parts of the world.

The locals of Bermuda would have been smiling, too. They beat the hapless USA by 113 runs to book their place in the Caribbean. The UAE kept their World Cup dreams alive with a 63-run victory over Uganda.

In the group B climax, Canada romped to a 160-run victory over PNG, to ensure their World Cup qualification and the Scots condemned the Netherlands to the anxieties of the four-team World Cup shoot out, where they would be joined by Namibia, who beat Oman.

In the first of the play-off matches, centuries from Zuiderent (107) and D van Bunge (137) kept the Dutch dream alive with an 89-run win over Denmark. In the second, Namibia were shocked by the UAE, who chased down 241 with four wickets and three overs in hand.

The date 11 July 2005 was an important one in Netherlands cricket history and Bas Zuiderent responded to the pressure. His unbeaten 116 guided them to a total of 287. In reply, the UAE slipped to 142 all out. The Netherlands may have done it the hard way, but they had reached the World Cup for the third time.

For the record, Scotland went on to beat Ireland in the final of the ICC Trophy, but five teams would have had every reason to celebrate as the tournament finished: they had all booked their place on cricket's biggest stage.

**Out with a bang:** Ed Joyce's final acts in Irish colours were memorable ones – he hit two centuries in the tournament, his last before switching allegiance to England.

# ICC TROPHY 2005, Staged in Ireland

## Group A

| | P | W | L | NR | T | PTS | NRR | FOR | AGAINST |
|---|---|---|---|---|---|---|---|---|---|
| Ireland* | 5 | 4 | - | 1 | - | 9 | +1.494 | 999/199.5 | 701/200 |
| Bermuda* | 5 | 3 | 1 | 1 | - | 7 | +0.695 | 995/200 | 856/200 |
| UAE | 5 | 2 | 2 | 1 | - | 5 | +0.432 | 818/200 | 731/199.5 |
| Denmark | 5 | 2 | 2 | 1 | - | 5 | -0.210 | 774/200 | 816/200 |
| Uganda | 5 | 1 | 3 | 1 | - | 3 | -1.047 | 647/197.4 | 864/200 |
| USA | 5 | - | 4 | 1 | - | 1 | -1.385 | 756/200 | 1021/197.4 |

## Group B

| | P | W | L | NR | T | PTS | NRR | FOR | AGAINST |
|---|---|---|---|---|---|---|---|---|---|
| Scotland* | 5 | 5 | - | - | - | 10 | +2.065 | 823/163.1 | 694/233 |
| Canada* | 5 | 4 | 1 | - | - | 8 | +0.789 | 1141/221 | 974/222.4 |
| Netherlands | 5 | 3 | 2 | - | - | 6 | +1.451 | 867/191.3 | 707/229.5 |
| Namibia | 5 | 2 | 3 | - | - | 4 | +0.418 | 1104/224.2 | 1035/229.5 |
| Papua NG | 5 | 1 | 4 | - | - | 2 | -2.201 | 608/224 | 775/157.4 |
| Oman | 5 | - | 5 | - | - | 0 | -2.727 | 545/224 | 903/175 |

* Qualified for the 2007 World Cup

## SEMI-FINALS

at The Hills Cricket Club Ground, on 9 July 2005
Bermuda 219 for 9 (50 overs) (DA Minors 53*)
Scotland 222 for 4 (46.5 overs) (CV English 75*, GM Hamilton 59)
Scotland won by six wickets

at Castle Avenue, Dublin, on 9 July 2005
Canada 238 for 9 (50 overs) (AC Botha 4 for 47)
Ireland 241 for 6 (49.2 overs) (PR Gillespie 64*)
Ireland won by four wickets

## FIFTH/SIXTH PLACE PLAY-OFF

at Castle Avenue, Dublin, on 11 July 2005
Netherlands 287 for 4 (50 overs) (B Zuiderent 116*, TBM de Leede 65, RN ten Doeschate 65*)
United Arab Emirates 142 (31.3 overs)
Netherlands won by 145 runs
Netherlands qualified for the 2007 World Cup

## FINAL

IRELAND v. SCOTLAND (50-over match)
13 JULY 2005, CASTLE AVENUE, DUBLIN
Result: Scotland won by 47 runs
Series: Scotland win the 2005 ICC Trophy
Toss: Ireland
Umpires: S Hameed (Indonesia) and AL Hill (New Zealand)
Man of the Match: RR Watson (Scotland)

### SCOTLAND

| | | | |
|---|---|---|---|
| PJC Hoffmann | c DI Joyce | b Mooney | 23 |
| DF Watts | run out (White) | | 55 |
| RR Watson | c White | b Johnston | 94 |
| CV English | c White | b Johnston | 20 |
| PJC Hoffmann | c DI Joyce | b Mooney | 23 |
| +CJO Smith | st Bray | b McCallan | 2 |
| DR Brown | c DI Joyce | b Cooke | 59 |
| GM Hamilton | c Morgan | b Cooke | 12 |
| DR Lockhart | not out | | 18 |
| GI Maiden | c DI Joyce | b Cooke | 11 |
| *CM Wright | not out | | 1 |
| Extras | (b 5, lb 4, w 20) | | 11 |
| Total | (8 wickets, 50 overs) | | 324 |
| DNB: JAR Blain | | | |

FoW: 1/37 (Hoffmann), 2/157 (Watts), 3/195 (English), 4/198 (Smith), 5/234 (Watson), 6/283 (Brown), 7/292 (Hamilton), 8/312 (Maiden).

| Bowling | O | M | R | W |
|---|---|---|---|---|
| Mooney | 7 | 0 | 62 | 1 |
| Johnston | 10 | 0 | 66 | 2 |
| Botha | 5 | 0 | 20 | 0 |
| Cooke | 9 | 1 | 70 | 3 |
| McCallan | 10 | 0 | 41 | 1 |
| White | 9 | 0 | 56 | 0 |

### IRELAND

| | | | |
|---|---|---|---|
| DI Joyce | c Smith | b Hoffmann | 1 |
| +JP Bray | c Watson | b Maiden | 70 |
| EJG Morgan | lbw | b Hoffmann | 4 |
| EC Joyce | c Watson | b Wright | 81 |
| PG Gillespie | c Hamilton | b Wright | 9 |
| DT Johnston | st Smith | b Maiden | 23 |
| AR White | lbw | b Wright | 0 |
| AC Botha | lbw | b Watson | 10 |
| *WK McCallan | c Wright | b Brown | 1 |
| PJK Mooney | not out | | 22 |
| G Cooke | not out | | 34 |
| Extras | (b 1, lb 5, w 6) | | 11 |
| Total | (9 wickets, 50 overs) | | 277 |

FoW: 1/6 (DI Joyce), 2/11 (Morgan), 3/148 (Bray), 4/179 (Gillespie), 5/185 (EC Joyce), 6/188 (White), 7/217 (Botha), 8/218 (McCallan), 9/222 (Johnston).

| Bowling | O | M | R | W |
|---|---|---|---|---|
| Hoffmann | 10 | 2 | 47 | 2 |
| Brown | 10 | 2 | 33 | 1 |
| Wright | 7 | 0 | 48 | 3 |
| Blain | 5 | 0 | 32 | 0 |
| Watson | 9 | 0 | 45 | 1 |
| Maiden | 9 | 0 | 56 | 2 |

## LEADING RUN-SCORERS

| Name | Mat | I | NO | Runs | HS | Ave | 100 | 50 |
|---|---|---|---|---|---|---|---|---|
| B Zuiderent (Netherlands) | 7 | 7 | 3 | 474 | 119 | 118.50 | 3 | 1 |
| EC Joyce (Ireland) | 5 | 5 | 1 | 399 | 115* | 99.75 | 2 | 2 |
| IS Billcliff (Canada) | 7 | 7 | 3 | 315 | 102* | 78.75 | 1 | 1 |
| JM Davison (Canada) | 7 | 7 | 0 | 312 | 125 | 44.57 | 1 | 2 |
| DLS van Bunge (Netherlands) | 7 | 7 | 1 | 291 | 137 | 48.50 | 1 | 1 |
| K Kamyuka (Uganda) | 5 | 5 | 1 | 246 | 126* | 61.50 | 1 | 2 |
| Khurram Khan (UAE) | 7 | 7 | 1 | 239 | 92 | 39.83 | - | 3 |
| SJ Massiah (USA) | 6 | 6 | 2 | 232 | 108* | 58.00 | 1 | 1 |
| JJ Tucker (Bermuda) | 7 | 6 | 1 | 232 | 132 | 46.40 | 1 | 1 |
| G Snyman (Bermuda) | 7 | 7 | 2 | 228 | 83* | 45.60 | - | 1 |

## LEADING WICKET-TAKERS

| Name | Mat | O | M | R | W | Ave | Best | 4w | 5w |
|---|---|---|---|---|---|---|---|---|---|
| PJC Hoffmann (Scotland) | 7 | 58.1 | 13 | 173 | 17 | 10.17 | 6-12 | - | 1 |
| E Schiferli (Netherlands) | 7 | 59.5 | 4 | 249 | 17 | 14.64 | 5-20 | 1 | 1 |
| RN ten Doeschate (Netherlands) | 6 | 33.5 | 4 | 146 | 15 | 9.73 | 4-18 | 2 | - |
| TM Hansen (Denmark) | 6 | 49.5 | 2 | 210 | 15 | 14.00 | 6-30 | - | 1 |
| KT Sandher (Canada) | 6 | 39.5 | 1 | 183 | 13 | 14.07 | 5-56 | - | 1 |
| SF Burger (Namibia) | 7 | 58 | 6 | 217 | 13 | 16.69 | 5-23 | - | 1 |
| HAG Anthony (USA) | 5 | 44.5 | 0 | 234 | 12 | 19.50 | 5-46 | - | 1 |
| DT Johnston (Ireland) | 6 | 50.3 | 1 | 253 | 12 | 21.08 | 3-39 | - | - |
| WF Stelling (Netherlands) | 7 | 46.2 | 9 | 163 | 11 | 14.81 | 5-30 | - | 1 |
| DR Brown (Scotland) | 6 | 49 | 11 | 178 | 11 | 16.18 | 4-15 | 1 | - |

# THE TEAMS

Sixteen teams will battle it out to be declared the world's best one-day cricketing nation. The favourites will be Australia, the defending champions, who have routed Pakistan and India, respectively, in the last two finals. However, the hosts, the West Indies, have started to show signs of returning to power, while South Africa and New Zealand, the two biggest under-achievers of the leading ICC nations, will fancy their chances, given a bit of luck and some impetus. For England, success, after losing in three finals, is somewhat overdue. Then there is Sri Lanka, whose penchant for positive cricket always gives them a chance. It would be a terrific performance if the other full members of the ICC, Zimbabwe and Bangladesh, even made it to the Super Eight, emulating semi-finalists Kenya four years ago. Of the other teams, Scotland, Canada and the Netherlands have played in the finals before but for Ireland and Bermuda this World Cup is a new adventure.

Ricky Ponting led Australia to victory in 2003 and the Green and Gold have remained the nation to beat in all forms of international cricket.

# AUSTRALIA

## One-day Masters

**Australia may be the most successful team in the tournament's history, but it hasn't always been plain sailing in the World Cup for the three-time champions. They still possess all the weapons to win again, but the squad is beginning to show its age.**

They made a bright start in the inaugural competition in England in 1975, demolishing the hosts in the semi-finals en route to the Lord's finale where the West Indies, and Clive Lloyd in particular, stopped them firmly in their tracks. Then, to add to the heightened sense of gloom enveloping cricket Down Under from the fallout of Kerry Packer and World Series cricket, Australia bombed in the following two World Cups, failing to get through the group stages on both occasions.

Enter Allan Border. He may have accepted the captaincy begrudgingly, but under his leadership steel was added to the team and the 1987 World Cup, staged in India and Pakistan, was the platform upon which the Australians first displayed the qualities that saw them set new standards in both forms of the game over the next 20 years. They marched through to the final in Calcutta, where they gained a sweet victory over the Old Enemy, England.

Australia made great hosts in 1992, but the team were as hospitable on the field as the tournament organizers were off it, and – to their horror – the pre-competition favourites failed to make it through the group stages.

By 1996, with opening bowler Glenn McGrath and leg-spinner Shane Warne cutting a swathe through world cricket, Australia returned to the subcontinent as everybody's pick to lift the trophy. Sri Lanka had other ideas, thrilling the watching millions with their new brand of attacking cricket as they overcame hurdle after hurdle and ended

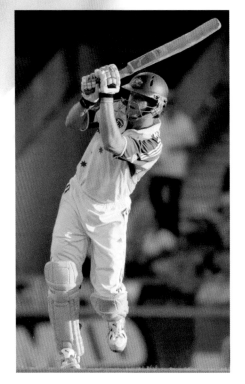

**Changing the game:** Adam Gilchrist's ability with bat and gloves have rendered specialist wicket-keepers almost redundant in one-day internationals.

Australian dreams in the final, winning by seven wickets with more than three overs in hand.

Three years later, Australia came to England as the best side in the world. Warne and McGrath were in their prime and wicket-keeper Adam Gilchrist was getting rave reviews as a swashbuckling opening batsman in the Jayasuriya mould. The Australians had reacted to Sri Lanka's 1996 success and had taken the one-day game to a new level. Their relentless march to success was almost halted at the semi-final stage where, to South Africa's immense disappointment, Lady Luck played a killing hand. With the scores level and with three balls remaining, Lance Klusener pushed a quick single and set off for the bowler's

end … where he met a stationary Allan Donald. Australia went through to the final by dint of having lost fewer wickets and, as if shaken into action, duly demolished Pakistan in the final at Lord's, skittling them for 132 and reaching their target in 20.1 overs.

They were shaken into action before a ball had even been bowled in South Africa in 2003. The news that Shane Warne had tested positive for a diuretic (the leg-spinner would be banned from all cricket for a year) sent shockwaves around the world, but if the Australians had been rattled by the incident, they certainly did not show it. They marched through the tournament untroubled and, inspired by Ricky Ponting's unbeaten 140, trounced India by 125 runs in the final.

### JOHN BUCHANAN

Buchanan cut his coaching teeth with Queensland and made his reputation by guiding them to their first Sheffield Shield title in 1994–95. Still, he was the surprise choice to succeed Geoff Marsh as Australia coach in 1999, but under his analytical command, Australian success has continued. He leaves the post following the World Cup.

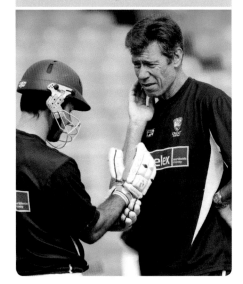

### WORLD CUP RECORD

| | | | |
|---|---|---|---|
| **1975** | runners-up | **1992** | group stages |
| **1979** | group stages | **1996** | runners-up |
| **1983** | group stages | **1999** | CHAMPIONS |
| **1987** | CHAMPIONS | **2003** | CHAMPIONS |

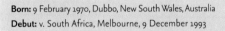
Australian fast bowlers to take up the challenge. There is no better example for them to follow than Brett Lee, who has used the one-day arena to relaunch his Test career. But he has lacked support. Left-armers Nathan Brackan and much-hyped prospect Mitchell Johnson or Queensland's warhorse Michael Kasprowicz, will all be vying to cement their place in the third-seamer role.

In contrast, the batting looks as solid as ever: Gilchrist is still a major weapon at the top of the order and can put a game beyond reach in just a few overs; Ricky Ponting remains prolific; Damien Martyn and Michael Hussey are very dependable run-makers; and Andrew Symonds is another who has pressed his Test claims with headline-grabbing one-day performances with both bat and ball. Australia will score enough runs; the question remains as to whether or not they can defend them.

The West Indies were the last team looking for a World Cup hat-trick. On that occasion they were shocked by India, the 66–1 rank outsiders: the defeat signalled the start of the West Indies' slide from dominance. Australia will be hoping history does not repeat itself. Their victory in the 2006 ICC Champions Trophy showed that the reigning champions are still the side to beat.

Since then, Australia have had a glimpse of life without Shane Warne, who announced his retirement from the one-day arena after his drugs ban, and Glenn McGrath, who, through a combination of injury and compassionate reasons, has played only 35 one-day internationals since Australia's 2003 success.

Whereas Australia have coped without Warne, their bowling looks increasingly vulnerable without their reliable metronomic opening bowler; as seen during the memorable Ashes summer of 2005 when England's two Test victories came when McGrath was missing through injury, and in Cape Town in March 2006 when he was once again absent and Australia failed to defend their world record one-day total of 434, with South Africa reaching the target with a ball to spare. McGrath's fitness may be vital to Australian hopes.

But the opening bowler will be 37 when the tournament starts and, coming as it does off the back of what will have been a demanding Ashes series, it is now time for a new generation of

## GLENN McGRATH

**Born:** 9 February 1970, Dubbo, New South Wales, Australia
**Debut:** v. South Africa, Melbourne, 9 December 1993
**Clubs:** New South Wales, Middlesex, Worcestershire
**Role:** Right-arm fast-medium bowler

### ODI STATISTICS

| | | | | | Batting | | | | | | | |
|---|---|---|---|---|---|---|---|---|---|---|---|---|
| Mat | inns | no | runs | hs | ave | sr | 100 | 50 | 4s | 6s | ct | st |
| 230 | 65 | 37 | 109 | 11 | 3.89 | 49.32 | 0 | 0 | 7 | 0 | 34 | 0 |

| | | | | | Bowling | | | | | |
|---|---|---|---|---|---|---|---|---|---|---|
| Mat | balls | runs | wkts | bb | ave | econ | sr | 4w | 5w | |
| 230 | 11983 | 7654 | 342 | 7/15 | 22.38 | 3.83 | 35.03 | 9 | 7 | |

**The greatest fast bowler of his time,** Glenn McGrath was plucked from virtual obscurity to take his place in Australia's Test line-up in 1993. He thrived: his height, pace and metronomic pursuit of the off-stump line have brought him more Test wickets than any other fast bowler in the game. His 7 for 15 against Namibia at the last World Cup is a tournament best and McGrath was the main reason that Australia coped so well with the absence of Shane Warne. With the 2007 World Cup following what will have been a tough Ashes campaign, the fitness of the 37-year-old will be crucial to Australian hopes..

# SOUTH AFRICA

## GROUP A
### The Under-achievers

The 1992 World Cup signalled the start of a bright new era for South African cricket. After 22 years of Apartheid-induced isolation, the Proteas were brought back in from the cricketing wilderness. And what an impact they made.

Through a combination of the searing pace of Allan Donald, the Jack-in-a-box fielding skills of gully Jonty Rhodes, and a string of fine all-round performances, they marched into the semi-finals. There, on an overcast night in Sydney, the rain-heavy clouds – rather than their opponents, England – brought their progress to a sickening halt. With South Africa needing 22 runs off 13 balls to secure a place in the final, the rain started to fall. When it stopped, the revised target was 21 off one ball. South Africa's World Cup was over.

## WORLD CUP RECORD

| | |
|---|---|
| 1992 semi-finals | 1999 semi-finals |
| 1996 quarter-finals | 2003 group stages |

**Flash and flair** Herschelle Gibbs's ability to score quickly gives South Africa the big starts that are so vital in the first few overs of an innings.

Gary Kirsten signalled his country's intent in the subcontinent in 1996, smashing a world record 188 not out against the United Arab Emirates, but South Africa's involvement ended in the quarter-finals, when Brian Lara's 111 inspired the West Indies to a 19-run victory.

When South Africa arrived at Edgbaston to play in the second semi-final of the 1999 World Cup in England, they would have been hoping that Lady Luck, who had so cruelly deserted them in Australia seven years earlier, would turn her gaze in their direction. But it was the inspired pace bowling of Shaun Pollock (5 for 36) and Allan Donald (4 for 32) that restricted Australia to 213 all out rather than any fortune. Faltering at 61 for 4 in the 21st over, Jacques Kallis and the effervescent Rhodes led the fightback, taking the Proteas to 175 for 6. Kallis's fall brought Lance Klusener to the crease: the hard-hitting all-rounder, who had made

## MICKEY ARTHUR

A dedicated and determined batsman who made the most of his ability to forge a successful first-class career for over a decade, Mickey Arthur took to coaching like a duck to water. However, despite success with the Eastern Cape side, his appointment as national coach in May 2005 still came as a surprise.

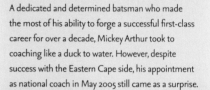

the tournament's biggest splash with his bruising strokeplay, smashed 31 off 16 balls to bring the scores level: then, someone, somewhere, lost their nerve. Allan Donald was run out with three balls remaining and the match was tied. Australia, having beaten South Africa in their Super Six encounter, progressed to the final.

Following the 1999 Edgbaston débâcle, and still reeling from the damaging revelations of former captain Hansie Cronje, South Africa played hosts in 2003 and were in desperate need of a World Cup pick-me-up. However, the tournament would be one of misery for the Rainbow Nation: they crashed out at the group stages.

Poor performances in their own backyard had exposed serious flaws in South African cricket. A scapegoat was needed and Shaun Pollock fitted the bill; he was dropped as captain, albeit retaining his place in the side, and 22-year-old Graeme

Smith took over the reins to become the country's youngest-ever captain.

The bright new dawn for South African cricket did not get off to the most auspicious of starts when they crashed to a 153-run defeat against India in a tri-nations tournament in Bangladesh; any signs of recovery were then quelled by England in the final of the NatWest Series when the Proteas were bowled out for 107 in just 32 overs – England had their hands on the trophy after just 20 overs...

A 3–2 series win against Pakistan, having been 2–0 down, signalled a change in South African fortunes, and that was confirmed with a 3–1 series win over the West Indies, with Kallis hitting two centuries.

But then the wheels came off against New Zealand. The disappointment of a 5–1 series defeat was compounded when South Africa were labelled cricket's official bad boys – the spectre of sledging had hung heavy over the series. The gloom was hardly lifted by a 5–0 reverse in Sri Lanka or by their failure to progress beyond the group stages of the 2004 ICC Champions Trophy in England.

## JACQUES KALLIS

**Born:** 16 October 1975, Cape Town, South Africa
**Debut:** v. England, Cape Town, 9 January 1996

**Clubs:** Western Province, Glamorgan, Middlesex
**Role:** Right-hand batsman, right-arm fast-medium bowler

### ODI STATISTICS

#### Batting

| Mat | inns | no | runs | hs | ave | sr | 100 | 50 | 4s | 6s | ct | st |
|---|---|---|---|---|---|---|---|---|---|---|---|---|
| 238 | 228 | 39 | 8159 | 139 | 43.16 | 70.28 | 13 | 57 | 619 | 99 | 92 | 0 |

#### Bowling

| Mat | balls | runs | wkts | bb | ave | econ | sr | 4w | 5w |
|---|---|---|---|---|---|---|---|---|---|
| 238 | 8348 | 6697 | 211 | 5/30 | 31.73 | 4.81 | 39.56 | 2 | 2 |

Until Andrew Flintoff arrived on the scene, Jacques Kallis was the game's best all-rounder. Building his batting success on a limpet-like quality to occupy the crease coupled with a sound technique and with the ability to generate a lively pace with the ball, his qualities were recognized when he was voted the ICC's Test and overall Player of the Year in 2005. One of only two players in the history of one-day international cricket to have scored 7,000 runs and taken 200 wickets, if Kallis can fire in the Caribbean, South Africa will be there or thereabouts come the end of the tournament.

## FORM GUIDE – Last 50 ODIs

| | |
|---|---|
| Won: | 30 |
| Lost: | 17 |
| Tied: | 1 |
| No result: | 2 |
| Winning percentage: | 63% |
| Highest score: | 438 (v. Australia, Jo'burg, 12 March 2006) |
| Lowest score: | 108 (v. New Zealand, Mumbai, 16 October 2006) |
| Most runs conceded: | 434 (v. Australia, Jo'burg, 12 March 2006) |
| Runs scored per 6 balls: | 5.04 |
| Runs conceded per 6 balls: | 4.81 |

## TOP FIVE PERFORMERS

- **Mark Boucher**, Border; RHB, WK; Born: 3 December 1976
- **Herschelle Gibbs**, Western Province; RHB; Born: 23 February 1974
- **Makhaya Ntini**, Border; RAF; Born: 6 July 1977
- **Shaun Pollock**, Natal; RHB, RAFM; Born: 16 July 1973
- **Graeme Smith**, Gauteng; LHB, SLA, captain; Born: 1 February 1981

However, it was England's arrival in the winter of 2004–05 that saw a significant upturn in South Africa's fortunes. Fighting off the best efforts of Kevin Pietersen, South Africa strolled to a 4–1 series victory, with both Graeme Smith and Kallis picking up two centuries.

The new-found momentum continued: Zimbabwe were put to the sword, 3–0, and South Africa travelled to the Caribbean full of confidence. Boeta Dippenaar was the hero, hitting 317 runs at 105.66 as the visitors ran out 5–0 series winners against the West Indies.

A comprehensive win against New Zealand (4–0) and a tie in India (2–2) preceded Australia's visit in 2005–06; South Africa produced morale-boosting performances. With the series tied at 2–2, and forced to chase down a world record total of 434 for victory, Herschelle Gibbs produced the necessary fireworks, smashing a brutal 175 to hand the Proteas a sensational win.

It is this sort of form they hope to take with them to the 2007 World Cup. Although the performances of Kallis, Smith and Gibbs with the bat and Pollock and Makhaya Ntini (who share more than 550 one-day wickets) with the ball will be crucial to their hopes, South Africa have added a much-needed consistency to their game. They can be one of the most destructive performers in the one-day arena and, on their day, are capable of beating anyone.

There is no question that South Africa can win, but they need to get Lady Luck on their side and avoid pushing the self-destruct button.

# SCOTLAND

## Second Time Lucky?

The chances are that Scotland did not enjoy their World Cup debut back in 1999. This time round, there is more cause for hope as the Scots travel to the Caribbean seeking their first World Cup victory. With greater experience than before, it is not an impossible dream.

Although first-class cricket has been played in Scotland since 1905, and despite numerous unfruitful appearances in the English Benson & Hedges and NatWest one-day competitions, cricket in Scotland did not really start to progress until a major organizational shake-up took place in 1996. When the dust had settled, the results were evident when Scotland finished third in the 1997 ICC Trophy in Malaysia and secured themselves a place in the 1999 World Cup, along with tournament winners Bangladesh and Kenya.

### PETER DRINNEN

Following a limited career for Queensland, for whom he made five first-class appearances, Drinnen decided against a future as a wicketkeeper-batsman and became a full-time coach. He was appointed as technical director of Scottish cricket in 2003 and then went on to replace Andy Moles as national coach in 2006.

It was a debut World Cup campaign Scotland would not enjoy. An opening six-wicket defeat to Australia at Worcester was followed by a 94-run defeat to Pakistan, although Gavin Hamilton – the then Yorkshire all-rounder who would go on to gain a solitary Test cap for England – raised spirits with a defiant 76.

But more disappointment was to follow in the guise of a dispiriting 22-run defeat to Bangladesh. With John Blain taking 4 for 37 to restrict Bangladesh to 185 for 9 on a tricky wicket at The Grange, Edinburgh, Scotland slid to 163 all out. Gavin Hamilton again impressed, this time hitting a resistant 63, but the Scots had lost what had realistically been their World Cup final.

With the wind no longer in their sails, they were destroyed by the West Indies in their next game at Leicester. Having wilted in the face of hostile fast bowling from Ambrose, Walsh and co., Scotland subsided to 68 all out and an eight-wicket defeat. They managed 1 only 21 against New Zealand at Edinburgh in their final game … it was never going to be enough to challenge the Kiwis, who strolled to victory. Scotland were out of the tournament and left to lick their wounds: Scottish cricket still had a long way to go.

They looked on the 2001 ICC Trophy in Canada as a chance to bounce back, but this campaign was another destined to end in disappointment. After losing out to Namibia on run-rate for a place in the final, Scotland faced the nerve-racking prospect of a play-off against Canada for a place in the 2003 World Cup. It was a chance to redeem themselves; an opportunity

### WORLD CUP RECORD

1999  group stages

### FORM GUIDE – Last 8 ODIs

| | |
|---|---|
| Played: | 8 |
| Won: | 1 |
| Lost: | 7 |
| Tied: | 0 |
| No result: | 0 |
| Winning percentage: | 12% |
| Highest score: | 203 (v. Pakistan, Edinburgh, 27 June 2006) |
| Lowest score: | 68 (v. West Indies, Leicester, 27 May 1999) |
| Most runs conceded: | 261 (v. Pakistan, Chester-le-Street, 20 May 1999) |
| Runs scored per 6 balls: | 3.73 |
| Runs conceded per 6 balls: | 4.89 |

for another shot on the biggest stage in cricket. They blew it, never recovering from the loss of three early wickets for 21 to set an inadequate total of 176. Canada cantered to the target with over ten overs to spare. For Scotland, it was an opportunity missed and a time to regroup.

They may not have been going to South Africa in 2003, but they were presented with an opportunity to progress in another competition. The team accepted a place in the second division of England's 45-over one-day league. Eight wins over the course of three seasons might not sound like a lot, but one of those victories came in the country's last-ever game in the competition. Scotland bowed out in style, completing an emphatic eight-wicket win over Derbyshire at Edinburgh, with Paul Hoffman excelling with 3 for 25. As they looked forward to the following year's ICC Trophy in Ireland, things appeared to be in good shape.

And it was a tournament to remember for the Scots. Bolstered by the return of Warwickshire's veteran all-rounder Dougie Brown, who has nine one-day international caps for England to his name, Scotland emphatically topped their group with five straight wins to qualify for the semi-finals. After restricting Bermuda to 219 for 9 off 50 overs – Hoffman again impressing with 3 for 28 – they eased to their target with three overs to spare and six wickets in hand. Mission one – securing a place in the 2007 World Cup – accomplished. Mission two: to win the ICC Trophy for the first time. They did; aided by Ryan Watson's timely 94, Scotland set Ireland a mammoth 324 to win. They never came close and the Scots won by 47 runs to join the likes of Sri Lanka, Zimbabwe and Bangladesh as tournament winners.

It was as though Scottish cricket had come of age. Fuelled by the belief handed to them following their ICC victory, Scotland took their place in the revamped C&G Trophy in 2006. Wins against Worcestershire (CJ Richards hitting an unbeaten 85), Northamptonshire (IA Moran impressing with 5 for 28) and Derbyshire (Ryan Watson smashing an unbeaten 28) meant that, for the first time, Scotland had not finished bottom of an English league table. Their improvement was for all to see, and was confirmed when the touring Pakistan team had to work hard for their five-wicket victory.

However, when the squad for the World Cup was announced seven months before the start of the tournament, it put Scotland's World Cup hopes firmly in perspective: mostly amateurs, the players needed the extra time to arrange for time off work. They will all be hoping for a Caribbean experience to remember, but whatever happens, Scottish cricket has come a long way and it is certainly going in the right direction.

## TOP FIVE PERFORMERS

- **John Blain**, Scotland; RHB, RAFM; Born: 4 January 1970
- **Gavin Hamilton**, Scotland; RHB, RAFM; Born: 16 September 1974
- **Dougie Brown**, Warwickshire; RHB, RAM; Born: 29 October 1969
- **Neil McCallum**, Scotland; RHB; Born: 22 November 1977
- **Paul Hoffman**, Scotland; RHB, RAMF; Born: 14 January 1970

## RYAN WATSON

**Born:** 12 November 1976, Salisbury, Zimbabwe
**Debut:** v. Pakistan, Edinburgh, 27 June 2006
**Clubs:** Scotland
**Role:** Right-hand bat, right-arm medium bowler

### ODI STATISTICS

Batting

| Mat | inns | no | runs | hs | ave | sr | 100 | 50 | 4s | 6s | ct | st |
|---|---|---|---|---|---|---|---|---|---|---|---|---|
| 3 | 3 | 0 | 137 | 80 | 45.66 | 96.47 | 0 | 1 | 20 | 2 | 2 | 0 |

Bowling

| Mat | balls | runs | wkts | bb | ave | econ | sr | 4w | 5w |
|---|---|---|---|---|---|---|---|---|---|
| 3 | 108 | 121 | 3 | 3/18 | 40.33 | 6.72 | 36.00 | 0 | 0 |

Zimbabwe-born Ryan Watson became the toast of Scotland when his 94 off 99 balls in the ICC Trophy final against Ireland in Dublin helped his side to success. Indeed, he finished the ICC tournament as Scotland's leading run scorer. Watson's reward, in the absence of injured skipper Craig Wright, was the Scotland captaincy for his country's one-day international against Pakistan. He flourished, hitting a fine 80 off 85 balls. Scotland may have lost the game, but Watson's growing reputation was enhanced. If Scotland do manage to break their World Cup duck, Ryan Watson will have played a full part in the action.

# NETHERLANDS

**Rank Outsiders**

Given that there are only 6,000 regular cricketers in the Netherlands and that the game is ranked as the country's 25th most popular sport, simply being at the 2007 World Cup will give the Dutch cause for cheer. But they have players who can leave their mark.

Although the history of Dutch cricket dates back to the 1850s, it took more than a century before their performances registered on the game's Richter scale. When they did, though, they managed to cause quite a tremor.

When the Australians – off the back of a hard-fought 1–0 Ashes triumph – visited The Hague on 29 April 1964, they came unstuck against an inspired Dutch side. Bill Lawry, Wally Grout, Graham Mackenzie & co. subsided to 197 all out and the Netherlands romped to their target with three overs to spare.

But the storm the victory had caused settled almost as quickly as it had been stirred, and what had been a staggering milestone in Dutch cricket led to little change. Restricted to one-off games against tourists to England, it wasn't until 1979 and the launch of the ICC Trophy that lesser

## TOP FIVE PERFORMERS

- **Tim de Leede**, Holland; RHB, RAM; Born: 25 January 1968
- **Billy Stelling**, Holland; RHB, RAFM; Born: 30 June 1969
- **Daan van Bunge**, Holland; RHB, LS; Born: 19 October 1982
- **Luuk van Troost**, Holland; LHB, LAM, captain; Born: 28 December 1969
- **Bas Zuiderent**, Holland; RHB, RAM; Born: 3 March 1977

## PETER CANTRELL

An attacking right-hand batsman and off-spin bowler who achieved moderate success with Queensland, Peter Cantrell first came to the Netherlands to coach Kampong Utrecht. He played for the Netherlands in the 1996 World Cup before going on to become their batting coach and then replaced Emerson Trotman as national coach in 2004.

cricketing nations, Holland among them, were provided with a suitable platform upon which to grow.

The Dutch failed to get beyond the group stages of the first two ICC tournaments, but came of age in 1986 in England, before losing out to Zimbabwe by 25 runs in the Lord's finale. They played hosts four years later – the first ICC Trophy to be played outside England – but lost out once again to Zimbabwe, who strolled to a six-wicket victory in the final at The Hague.

But there were still plenty of moments for celebration: a five-wicket victory over the West Indies in 1991 was followed by further victories over England (by seven wickets) in 1993 and South Africa (by nine wickets) in 1994. As a result, the Netherlands took their place in the 1994 ICC Trophy in Kenya with some confidence.

On the face of it, a third-place finish may seem like a downturn in fortunes, but the Netherlands' prize for beating Bermuda in a play-off was their biggest in cricket to date: it ensured their qualification for the 1996 World Cup in the subcontinent.

It turned out to be a tournament to forget. Heavy losses to New Zealand (by 119 runs), England (49 runs), Pakistan (eight wickets) and

**Big hope:** Bas Zuiderent caught the eye when he played in the 1996 World Cup as a teenager and he has since enjoyed a successful career in English county cricket.

the UAE (seven wickets) left the Dutch without a point and rooted to the bottom of their group table. It left no one involved with Dutch cricket in any doubt that they still had a long way to go.

Confidence was gained with a second-place finish in the inaugural European Championships later in the year and the Netherlands arrived in Malaysia for the 1997 ICC Trophy in good shape. They started well, coming through the opening group stage unbeaten, but then crashed

## FORM GUIDE – Last 17 ODIs

| | |
|---|---|
| Played: | 17 |
| Won: | 1 |
| Lost: | 15 |
| Tied: | 0 |
| No result: | 1 |
| Winning percentage: | 6% |
| Highest score: | 314 (v. Namibia, Bleomfontein, 3 March 2003) |
| Lowest score: | 86 (v. Sri Lanka, Colombo, 16 September 2002) |
| Most runs conceded: | (v.) |
| Runs scored per 6 balls: | 4.09 |
| Runs conceded per 6 balls: | 5.87 |

looked as though it was going to be another World Cup to forget when the Dutch fell to five straight defeats in South Africa when it came to the real thing. However, pride was restored in their final game when they recorded a comfortable 64-run win over Namibia, with both Feiko Kloppenburg (121) and Klaas-Jan van Noortwijk (134 not out) hitting form as the Dutch hammered 314 – their record one-day total.

A fifth-place finish in the 2005 ICC Trophy was enough to ensure them all-important qualification for the 2007 World Cup and, what's more, granted them one-day international status until the 2009 ICC Trophy. Their 2006 form has been patchy, suffering two heavy defeats at the hands of the Sri Lankans and a disappointing reverse against their Group A World Cup opponents Scotland in the European Championships.

Expectations for the Caribbean might not be high, but the Dutch will still be bitterly disappointed if they leave the tournament without a win. With a couple of players now full-time professionals in England, and thus playing regular limited-overs cricket, one victory is not an unreasonable target.

to two defeats in the next phase and their misery was compounded by a three-wicket defeat to Denmark in the fifth-place play-off. The Netherlands had comprehensively missed out on a place in the 1999 World Cup.

It was time for them to rebuild and there was no better place for them to do so than in the English NatWest Trophy. Having entered the competition in 1995, their best performance came in 1999 when they reached the fourth round, beating Durham along the way. A new generation of Dutch cricketers were now starting to benefit from regular match-ups with first-class cricketers.

And the benefits of these experiences manifested themselves in the 2001 ICC Trophy staged in Canada. Having qualified comfortably for the Super League stage, they won five out of their next six games to qualify for the final, where they would meet the only team to have beaten them in the tournament so far, Namibia. In a thrilling, mesmerizing contest, the Netherlands clawed themselves back from the brink of defeat to earn a dramatic last-ball victory. It provided them with their greatest day in cricket and handed them another shot at the World Cup.

Two heavy defeats to Sri Lanka and Pakistan in the pre-World Cup work-out in the 2002 Champions Trophy did not bode well, and it

## RYAN TEN DOESCHATE

**Born:** 30 June 1980, Port Elizabeth, South Africa
**Debut:** v.. Sri Lanka, Amstelveen, 4 July 2006
**Clubs:** Western Province, Essex
**Role:** Right-hand bat, right-arm medium-fast bowler

### ODI STATISTICS

#### Batting

| Mat | inns | no | runs | hs | ave | sr | 100 | 50 | 4s | 6s | ct | st |
|---|---|---|---|---|---|---|---|---|---|---|---|---|
| 2 | 2 | 1 | 95 | 56* | 95.00 | 130.13 | 0 | 1 | 10 | 4 | 0 | 0 |

#### Bowling

| Mat | balls | runs | wkts | bb | ave | econ | sr | 4w | 5w |
|---|---|---|---|---|---|---|---|---|---|
| 2 | 60 | 86 | 3 | 2/51 | 28.66 | 8.60 | 20.00 | 0 | 0 |

Born in South Africa, Ryan ten Doeschate decided to make the most of his Dutch descent and grabbed the opportunity to represent the country of his ancestors in the 2007 World Cup. In addition, his EC passport allowed him to forge a career in county cricket, and, after impressing in a pre-season game against Essex, he duly signed for the southeast county. He may have had to work hard for a place in the championship team, but the hard-hitting batsman and medium-pace bowler has flourished in the one-day arena and played a match-winning role in his side's win over Middlesex – hitting 51 off 41 balls – as Essex marched to the 2005 National League title.

## WORLD CUP RECORD

1996 group stages      2003 group stages

# SRI LANKA

## GROUP B
### Inventors of the One-day Game

**When Sri Lanka clinched the trophy in 1996 they shocked the cricket world and with a few of the old guard seeking one last hurrah, they will be looking to pull off a similar surprise in the Caribbean.**

Sri Lanka's first taste of international cricket was a bitter one. Facing the might of the West Indies, they were blown away by the Caribbean battery of fast bowlers and slipped to 86 all out. They fared little better against Pakistan, making a paltry 138 chasing a mammoth 331 for victory.

They went to England in the summer of 1979 hopeful, rather than expectant, of qualification to the World Cup proper via the inaugural ICC Trophy that preceded it. They were too strong for the lesser cricketing nations, romping through

**Leading from the front:** A veteran of more than 220 one-day internationals and with eight centuries to his name, new captain Mahela Jayawardene is in a rich vein of form.

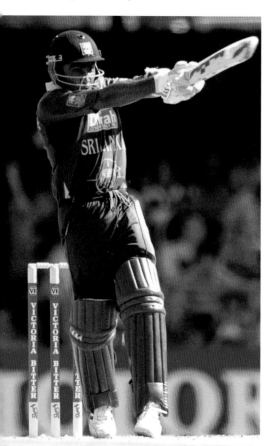

the tournament and beating Canada by 60 runs in the final. Their World Cup qualification was ensured.

And it was here, in the 1979 World Cup, that the world first gained a glimpse of the Sri Lankans' raw potential. They failed to progress beyond the group stages, but they returned to the subcontinent having gained a major scalp. Following a heavy loss to New Zealand and a washout against the West Indies, they recorded the biggest win in their history when they beat India by 47 runs. The result caused a nation to dance in the streets.

That win contributed to Sri Lanka's elevation to Test status in 1981, and they entered the 1983 World Cup as one of cricket's big boys. Although they departed from the competition following the group stages once again, their solitary win against New Zealand meant that they left with their heads held high.

Which is more than can be said following their performances four years later, as the Cricket World Cup made it to the subcontinent for the first time. Sri Lanka made the short trip home without a single win to their name.

Things improved slightly in 1992 as Sri Lanka notched up two World Cup victories for the first

### TOP FIVE PERFORMERS

- **Kumar Sangakkara**, Nondescripts CC; LHB, WK; Born: 27 October 1977
- **Mahela Jayawardene**, Sinhalese Sports Club; RHB, RAM, captain; Born: 27 May 1977
- **Chaminda Vaas**, Colts CC; LHB, LAFM; Born: 27 January 1974
- **Sanath Jayasuriya**, Colombo CC; LHB, SLA; Born: 30 June 1969
- **Lasith Malinga**, Galle CC; RHB, RAFM; Born: 28 August 1983

### FORM GUIDE – Last 50 ODIs

| | |
|---|---|
| Won: | 26 |
| Lost: | 22 |
| Tied: | 0 |
| No result: | 2 |
| Winning percentage: | 54% |
| Highest score: | 443 (v. Netherlands, Amstelveen, 4 July 2006) |
| Lowest score: | 122 (v. India, Chandigarh, 28 October 2005) |
| Most runs conceded: | 368 (v. Australia, Sydney, 12 February 2006) |
| Runs scored per 6 balls: | 5.25 |
| Runs conceded per 6 balls: | 4.95 |

time: first against New Zealand and then, more significantly, against South Africa, but despite these brief moments of cheer, Sri Lanka had fallen at the first hurdle once again.

And it is for all the above reasons that their performances in the 1996 World Cup shocked the cricketing world. It wasn't just the fact they won the competition, it was the style in which they did so that left millions watching with awe. Using the newly introduced 15-over fielding restrictions to their advantage, they simply blitzed their opponents.

Against the threat of terrorism on their island, Sri Lanka cruised through the group stages with a record reading played five, won five. Two of those "victories" had come via forfeits – given the tense political situation, Australia and the West Indies refused to play in Colombo – but the manner of their three victories left people talking, particularly their six-wicket demolition of India, in which opener Sanath Jayasuriya had smashed a 76-ball 79.

England were no match for Sri Lanka in the quarter-finals, with Jayasuriya this time hammering 82 off 44 balls. Next up were India

## MUTTIAH MURALITHARAN

**Born:** 17 April 1972, Kandy, Sri Lanka
**Debut:** v. India, Colombo, 12 August 1993

**Clubs:** Tamil Union Cricket & Athletic Club, Kent, Lancashire
**Role:** Right-hand batsman, right-arm off-break bowler

### ODI STATISTICS

#### Batting

| Mat | inns | no | runs | hs | ave | sr | 100 | 50 | 4s | 6s | ct | st |
|-----|------|-----|------|-----|------|-------|-----|-----|-----|-----|-----|-----|
| 282 | 132 | 49 | 480 | 27 | 5.78 | 69.86 | 0 | 0 | 31 | 6 | 112 | 0 |

#### Bowling

| Mat | balls | runs | wkts | bb | ave | econ | sr | 4w | 5w |
|-----|-------|------|------|------|-------|------|-------|-----|-----|
| 282 | 15397 | 9866 | 425 | 7/30 | 23.21 | 3.84 | 36.22 | 11 | 8 |

One of the most successful bowlers in the history of the game, Muttiah Muralitharan has also been one of the most controversial. His bent-arm bowling action – no-balled on several occasions and subsequently cleared by the ICC – allows him to impart tremendous spin on the ball and he has become one of the most deadly spin bowlers in the game. In May 2004, he overtook Courtney Walsh's haul of 519 to become the leading wicket taker in Test history. Shane Warne has since overhauled him, but Muralitharan seems destined to pass the 700-wicket mark. He remains a vital cog in Sri Lanka's machinery.

## TOM MOODY

Considered a one-day specialist – he won the World Cup with Australia in 1987 and 1999 – Tom Moody could not establish himself in Australia's all-conquering Test side of the late 1980s and early '90s. After a prolific 15-year first-class career, he turned to coaching, first with Worcestershire and then, in May 2005, with Sri Lanka.

and, with the home side floundering on 120 for 8 (chasing 252 for victory), the crowd's frustrations evolved into a near riot; with sections of the Eden Gardens stands ablaze and massed riot police taking their positions, the match was abandoned. Sri Lanka were awarded the game and a place in the final.

The fun did not stop there: aided by a brilliant century from Aravinda de Silva (107 not out), Sri Lanka eased to a seven-wicket victory against Australia to earn the right to be called the one-day world champions. Their style of play revolutionized the way that one-day cricket is played and that one-day cricket is now the game's biggest money-spinner and enjoyed by millions is down in no small part to Sri Lanka; there could be no higher compliment.

All of which made their failure to progress beyond the group stages in England in 1999 all the more disappointing. They salvaged their reputation in South Africa four years later when they reached the semi-finals before losing to eventual winners Australia by 48 runs.

That tournament signalled the end of the road for de Silva. Arjuna Ranatunga had gone before

him; it was now time for a new generation of cricketers – led by Jayasuriya and the phenomenal Muttiah Muralitharan – to lead Sri Lanka into the future.

Their failure to progress beyond the group stages of the 2004 Champions Trophy was more like a blast from the past, but confidence was boosted by two successive cup wins, over Pakistan and India respectively.

A 3–0 series win over Bangladesh was followed by a sterner test in India. Sri Lanka were found wanting, slipping to a 6–1 series defeat. Things got no better in New Zealand, where they fell to a 4–1 reverse. But improved performances in Australia and a home series win over Bangladesh heralded a return to form and that was confirmed when they whitewashed a woeful England 5–0 during the summer of 2006 and followed that by hammering a world record 443 against the Netherlands.

Not many people will be putting money on Sri Lanka to repeat their 1996 success, but you discount any team containing the likes of the explosive Jayasuriya and the mercurial Muralitharan at your peril.

### WORLD CUP RECORD

| | | | |
|------|--------------|------|--------------|
| 1975 | group stages | 1992 | group stages |
| 1979 | group stages | 1996 | CHAMPIONS |
| 1983 | group stages | 1999 | group stages |
| 1987 | group stages | 2003 | semi-finals |

# INDIA

**A Nation Expects**

Ever since India first lifted the trophy in 1983 they have been serial contenders for the Cricket World Cup, but as far as their passionate supporters are concerned, nothing short of victory for their team will do.

Although World Cup success had been limited in India's first two tournament appearances, they hit an all-time low when they suffered a chastening loss to minnows Sri Lanka in 1979. Chasing 239 for victory, India subsided to a sorry 191 all out. Their World Cup dream was over and they returned home in disgrace.

To understand Indian cricket is to understand the frenzied passion of that country's supporters, and when India's cricketers returned to England for the 1983 World Cup they not only had a point to prove but an entire nation to appease. They may have been rank 66–1 outsiders when the tournament started, but when it finished, they had millions of their fanatical supporters cheering in the streets.

Every success story needs a hero and young all-rounder Kapil Dev was more than willing to play the leading role. Having won two and lost two of their opening games, India's World Cup dreams were hanging by a thread when they slipped to 17 for 5 against Zimbabwe. Kapil Dev had other ideas, smashing a spectacular 138-ball 175 to rescue his side and haul their total to 266. Zimbabwe were then duly dismissed for 235.

With confidence restored, India thrashed Australia by 118 runs in their final group match to secure their place in the semi-final at Old Trafford. Kapil Dev shone with the ball this time, taking 3 for 35 as England subsided to a disappointing 213 all out. India cantered to the victory target with six wickets and five overs to spare.

India had already played the West Indies twice in the tournament, with one win apiece, but the Caribbean giants, seeking a hat-trick of World Cup wins, were the firm favourites to lift the trophy. And all the pre-match predictions seemed accurate when India fell to a disappointing 183 all out. But their bowlers rose to the challenge, scything through the West Indies' batting line-up to dismiss them for 140. India had won by 43 runs: a nation erupted with joy.

There was no better place for the World Cup circus to pitch its tent than India and Pakistan in 1987. England may be the historical home of cricket, but the subcontinent remains the true spiritual centre of the game. And how the crowds cheered as India, after suffering an opening one-run defeat to Australia, won their next five games

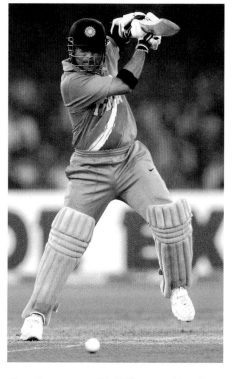

**The Little Master:** Once labelled by Sir Donald Bradman as his "modern incarnation", Sachin Tendulkar is a legend of the modern game.

to book a place in the semi-finals. However, in front of a full house in Bombay, England ended India's World Cup reign with a 35-run victory. Any disappointment at that defeat was intensified four years later when India won only two of their eight group games and were sent packing from the tournament at the first hurdle.

They made it through to the semi-finals when the World Cup returned to the subcontinent in 1996; this time they would face Sri Lanka. India's island neighbours may have been the tournament's surprise package, but India were the strong favourites and, what's more, their supporters demanded victory. So when their side capitulated to 120 for 8 chasing 252 for victory,

## GREG CHAPPELL

Greg Chappell was the outstanding Australian batsman of his generation and someone with an impeccable sense of timing. He scored centuries in both the first and last of his 87 Tests and back-to-back centuries the first of his 48 Tests as captain. He was appointed India's coach in May 2005.

## WORLD CUP RECORD

| | | | |
|---|---|---|---|
| **1975** | group stages | **1992** | group stages |
| **1979** | group stages | **1996** | semi-finals |
| **1983** | CHAMPIONS | **1999** | Super Six |
| **1987** | semi-finals | **2003** | runners-up |

## FORM GUIDE – Last 50 ODIs

| | |
|---|---|
| Won: | 26 |
| Lost: | 22 |
| Tied: | 0 |
| No result: | 2 |
| Winning percentage: | 54% |
| Highest score: | 350 (v. Sri Lanka, Nagpur, 25 October 2005) |
| Lowest score: | 144 (v. Pakistan, Delhi, 17 April 2005) |
| Most runs conceded: | 319 (v. Pakistan, Ahmedabad, 12 April 2005) |
| Runs scored per 6 balls: | 5.17 |
| Runs conceded per 6 balls: | 4.99 |

the 100,000-strong Eden Gardens crowd were less than enamoured. Bottles were thrown, fires were started and, by the time a near riot had erupted, Sri Lanka had been awarded the game. India's World Cup dreams were over yet again.

Failure to reach the knock-out phases in England in 1999 would have done little to appease the discontent of a success-craving public, but India's march to the final in South Africa allowed a nation to dream again. But Ricky Ponting halted any plans for a victory parade, hitting an unbeaten 140 as Australia romped to their second successive title.

India enjoyed mixed post-World Cup fortunes, but the highs of a thrilling series win over Pakistan in 2004 were matched by the lows of an early exit from the Champions Trophy later in the year and a 4–2 home series defeat against Pakistan in 2005. It was time for a change: Rahul Dravid was appointed captain and, under new coach Greg Chappell, a new era in Indian cricket had begun.

## TOP FIVE PERFORMERS

- **Mahendra Dhoni**, Jharkhand; RHB, WK; Born: 7 July 1981
- **Harbhajan Singh**, Punjab; RHB, OS; Born: 3 July 1980
- **Irfan Pathan**, Baroda; LHB, LAMF; Born: 27 October 1984
- **Virender Sehwag**, Delhi; RHB, OS; Born: 20 October 1978
- **Sachin Tendulkar**, Mumbai; RHB, LS; Born: 24 April 1973

## RAHUL DRAVID

**Born:** 11 January 1973, Indore, India
**Debut:** v. Sri Lanka, Singapore, 3 April 1996
**Clubs:** Karnataka, Scotland, Kent
**Role:** Right-hand bat, right-arm off-break bowler, occasional wicketkeeper, captain

### ODI STATISTICS

| Mat | inns | no | runs | hs | ave | sr | 100 | 50 | 4s | 6s | ct | st |
|---|---|---|---|---|---|---|---|---|---|---|---|---|
| | | | | | Batting | | | | | | | |
| 300 | 279 | 35 | 9681 | 153 | 39.67 | 70.50 | 12 | 71 | 848 | 29 | 180 | 14 |

| Mat | balls | runs | wkts | bb | ave | econ | sr | 4w | 5w |
|---|---|---|---|---|---|---|---|---|---|
| | | | | Bowling | | | | | |
| 300 | 186 | 170 | 4 | 2/43 | 42.50 | 5.48 | 46.50 | 0 | 0 |

Nicknamed "The Wall" by his team-mates in the early part of his Test career because of his obduracy, Rahul Dravid has developed into one of the most classically elegant run-scorers in the game. He truly came of age in Calcutta in 2001 when he scored 180 in India's memorable win over Australia and has been prolific ever since, the highlight coming when he scored a faultless 270 in Pakistan in 2004. He was appointed captain of the one-day side in October 2005 and soon took over the reins of the Test team. He has already established his place in the pantheon of Indian greats.

The players responded well. Any pain suffered following a loss in the final of a tri-nation tournament in Zimbabwe to New Zealand was eased by a 6–1 home series win over Sri Lanka, with wicketkeeper Mahendra Dhoni impressing with the bat. Further series wins over Pakistan and England boosted their one-day standing, and India went to the Caribbean for a World Cup dress rehearsal full of hope. They suffered stage fright, losing 4–1, and will be hoping that result isn't an omen of things to come by the time the World Cup proper comes around.

# BANGLADESH

**Minnows Demanding Respect**

They may have been part of the Test match scene for seven years, but Bangladesh remain one of the minnows of the world game. However, as they have proved on a few occasions, even the minnows can have their day.

The decision to grant Bangladesh Test status in 2000 was a controversial one. The critics clamoured they were too weak to play in the upper echelon of world cricket; the negative voices grew in volume after they had lost 31 out of their first 35 Test matches.

They broke their Test match duck in 2005, recording a comprehensive 222-run win against Zimbabwe in Chittagong. The victory sparked scenes of jubilation across the cricket-mad country.

This may remain their only Test win to date, but those shouting previously had either a short memory or a profound ignorance of cricket history. India had taken time to adjust to life with the established teams and New Zealand had taken 27 years to record their first Test victory.

Bangladesh's journey to the higher reaches of the world game has not been an easy one. Eight years after the country gained its independence from Pakistan after the bloody Bangladesh Liberation War, they had their first taste of international cricket, in the inaugural ICC Trophy in England in 1979. And only a nail-biting ten-run defeat against Denmark in their final group game prevented them from progressing to the knock-out stages.

## WORLD CUP RECORD

| | |
|---|---|
| **1999** group stages | **2003** group stages |

They made progress four years later as they marched through the group stages, before they came unstuck against Zimbabwe in the semi-finals. Deflated, they lost the third/fourth play-off as well.

The 1986 tournament ended in bitter disappointment, when only Argentina finished below them in their seven-team group, but they bounced back in the Netherlands four years later until they ran into Zimbabwe in the semi-finals once again: this time the Africans coasted to an 84-run victory.

However, the defining moment in Bangladesh's cricket history to that point came in Malaysia in 1997. They raced through the competition unbeaten to reach the semi-finals once again. But it was third time lucky as they beat Scotland by 72 runs with Mohammad Rafique taking 4 for 25.

In a nail-biting rain-affected final, they beat Kenya by two wickets. It was a seminal moment and, most important of all, it ensured Bangladesh's qualification for the 1999 World Cup in England. It was a chance to test themselves against the giants of the game.

They got off to an inauspicious start, losing to New Zealand by six wickets after sliding to 116 all out. They fared little better against the West Indies, with Courtney Walsh taking 4 for 25 as Bangladesh fell to 182 all out and the West Indies ran out seven-wicket winners.

**Flamboyant and explosive:** Test match cricket's youngest ever centurion, Mohammad Ashraful's brilliantly paced century at Cardiff set up a memorable one-day win over Australia in 2005.

## TOP FIVE PERFORMERS

- **Habibul Bashar**, Biman Bangladesh; RHB, OS; Born: 17 August 1972
- **Javed Omar**, Dhaka Division; RHB, LS; Born: 25 November 1976
- **Khaled Mashud**, Rajshahi Division; RHB, WK; Born: 8 February 1976
- **Mohammad Ashraful**, Dhaka Division; RHB, LS; Born: 7 July 1984
- **Mohammad Rafique**, Dhaka Division; LHB, SLA; Born: 9 May 1970

## FORM GUIDE – Last 50 ODIs

| | |
|---|---|
| Won: | 17 |
| Lost: | 33 |
| Tied: | 0 |
| No result: | 0 |
| Winning percentage: | 34% |
| Highest score: | 301 (v. Kenya, Bogra, 17 March 2006) |
| Lowest score: | 86 (v. New Zealand, Chittagong, 2 November 2004) |
| Most runs conceded: | 391 (v. England, Trent Bridge, 21 June 2005) |
| Runs scored per 6 balls: | 4.37 |
| Runs conceded per 6 balls: | 4.75 |

## MUSHRAFE MORTAZA

**Born:** 5 October 1983, Norail, Jessore, Bangladesh   **Clubs:** Bangladesh
**Debut:** v. Zimbabwe, Chittagong, 23 November 2001   **Role:** Right-hand batsman, right-arm fast-medium bowler

### ODI STATISTICS

#### Batting

| Mat | inns | no | runs | hs | ave | sr | 100 | 50 | 4s | 6s | ct | st |
|---|---|---|---|---|---|---|---|---|---|---|---|---|
| 44 | 36 | 7 | 439 | 44* | 15.13 | 98.43 | 0 | 0 | 41 | 12 | 12 | 0 |

#### Bowling

| Mat | balls | runs | wkts | bb | ave | econ | sr | 4w | 5w |
|---|---|---|---|---|---|---|---|---|---|
| 44 | 2259 | 1785 | 56 | 6/26 | 31.87 | 4.74 | 40.33 | 1 | 1 |

Mushrafe Mortaza made his debut for Bangladesh in a one-day game against Zimbabwe at Chittagong in 2001 – it was his first first-class match. Tall, fast and aggressive, he has curbed his natural inclination to bang the ball in short and has become a reliable fast-medium line and length bowler. His breakthrough in the Test arena came against England in 2003–04 when he took 4 for 60 in the first innings, but a twisted knee in the second innings saw him out of action for a year. He confirmed his return to fitness by taking 6 for 26 in Bangladesh's comprehensive win over Kenya in Nairobi in August 2006.

But if ever Bangladesh had a chance to record their first ever World Cup victory, then it came against Scotland, a side they had beaten en route to their 1997 ICC Trophy success. They repeated the trick, coming out on top in a low-scoring match by 22 runs.

They were then taught a cricket lesson by Australia, who reached their victory target of 179 in just 195 balls, with Adam Gilchrist blasting a 39-ball 63.

To round off their opening World Cup campaign, Bangladesh faced their biggest match of the tournament. In front of a packed Northampton crowd, bolstered by partisan

## DAV WHATMORE

Born in Sri Lanka but brought up in Australia, Whatmore enjoyed a prolific first-class career with Victoria – rewarded by seven Test caps – before he turned to coaching. The highlight came when he led the country of his birth to World Cup success in 1996. He was appointed coach of a struggling Bangladesh side in 2003.

members from both communities in England, this was cricket's version of David and Goliath, a match with attitude between two nations who shared an acrimonious past. True to fairytale form, Bangladesh defeated Pakistan by 62 runs.

It is a result laced with irony on many levels. It was the biggest win in Bangladesh's cricket history and almost certainly accelerated their elevation to Test status. But it is also a match deeply associated with the dark side of the game, coming as it did under intense scrutiny during the black days of match fixing.

The Test tag seemed to hang as heavily around their shoulders in the one-day arena as it did for them in Tests. Victories came sporadically and when you see against whom they achieved the majority of those successes – eight wins against Kenya and six against Zimbabwe – it puts their plight into perspective.

The 2003 World Cup in South Africa may have come and gone without Bangladesh having caused much of a stir – they failed to win a game – but there have been moments of cheer for their followers.

One of these came when they beat India by 15 runs on Boxing Day 2004 in Dhaka; another was when they shocked the Australians in Cardiff in 2005. Set 250 for an unlikely victory, Mohammad Ashraful's century inspired them to a five-wicket victory with three balls to spare. And a win over Sri Lanka in February 2006 furthered the belief that the fortunes of Bangladesh cricket are on the up.

It is difficult to know what would represent progress for Bangladeshi cricket, but a place in the Super Eight is certainly not beyond their capabilities.

# BERMUDA

## GROUP B
### World Cup Debutants

**Bermuda's build-up to their first World Cup appearance has been anything but smooth but, despite the misfortune of having been drawn in a difficult group, they will still be looking to savour their first experience of the Cricket World Cup.**

The first records of cricket in Bermuda, a group of 138 islands in the North Atlantic, came in 1844. But international appearances were limited. There are records of touring teams from the United States, and they played sporadic games against international teams who were on their way to the West Indies.

They joined the ICC in 1960 and took their place in the line-up for the inaugural ICC Trophy in 1979, a tournament that had been proposed by Alma Hunt, Bermuda's delegate to the ICC. They marched through to the semi-finals, before they came unstuck against Canada.

**Bermuda Triangle:** All-rounder Janeiro Tucker captained the Bermudan cricket team to victory over Canada in their first-ever one-day international in May 2006. Will any of his opponents in Group B go missing?

Bermuda went one better in 1982 when they reached the final. However, Zimbabwe put a halt on any dreams of victory when they won by three wickets. The Africans were their nemesis four years later, but this time in the semi-final stage.

Bermuda were unlucky to be paired in the same group as Bangladesh and Kenya in the ICC Trophy in the Netherlands in 1990 and, following defeats to both, departed the competition after the group stages for the first time.

They recovered in Kenya four years later, before falling to the hosts at the semi-final stage, but lost ground in Malaysia in 1997, when they failed to progress beyond the group stages, a performance they repeated in Canada in 2001.

The mood of Bermuda's players was hardly lifted in February 2005 following the

appointment of former Bermuda Cricket Board president and ex-player El James as national coach. More than one player voiced concerns over his management technique and the team went to the ICC Trophy tournament in Ireland with storm clouds brewing over their heads.

They put any differences aside and performed admirably. After an initial 97-run defeat in their opening game against the hosts, they recorded successive wins against the UAE and Denmark. A no result against Uganda meant that if they won their final group game against the United States they would not only qualify for the semi-final but

### WORLD CUP RECORD

World Cup debutants

## FORM GUIDE – Last 5 ODIs

| | |
|---|---|
| Played: | 5 |
| Won: | 3 |
| Lost: | 2 |
| Tied: | 0 |
| No result: | 0 |
| Winning percentage: | 60% |
| Highest score: | 272 (v. Canada, Toronto, 21 August 2006) |
| Lowest score: | 145 (v. Zimbabwe, Port of Spain, 18 May 2006) |
| Most runs conceded: | 338 (v. Zimbabwe, Port of Spain, 18 May 2006) |
| Runs scored per 6 balls: | 3.89 |
| Runs conceded per 6 balls: | 4.87 |

## IRVINE ROMAINE

**Born:** 8 August 1972, Bermuda
**Debut:** v. Canada, Port of Spain, 17 May 2006

**Clubs:** Bermuda
**Role:** Right-hand batsman, right-arm off-break bowler

### ODI STATISTICS

Batting

| Mat | inns | no | runs | hs | ave | sr | 100 | 50 | 4s | 6s | ct | st |
|---|---|---|---|---|---|---|---|---|---|---|---|---|
| 5 | 4 | 0 | 211 | 101 | 52.75 | 70.56 | 1 | 1 | 26 | 5 | 2 | 0 |

Bowling

| Mat | balls | runs | wkts | bb | ave | econ | sr | 4w | 5w |
|---|---|---|---|---|---|---|---|---|---|
| 5 | 90 | 78 | 3 | 2/22 | 26.00 | 5.20 | 30.00 | 0 | 0 |

An integral part of the Bermuda side that finished fourth in the 2005 ICC Tournament that ensured his side's place in the 2007 World Cup, Irvine Romaine was appointed captain and has since led by example. He made the headlines in April 2006 when he smashed 59 off an England representative side in Port of Spain and kept his form as Bermuda warmed up for the World Cup by hitting 62 out of his side's sorry all-out total of 144 against Zimbabwe. He followed that up with a sparkling knock of 101 against Canada in Toronto in August 2006 to lead his side to a morale-boosting 11-run victory.

would also secure a place in the 2007 World Cup.

Thursday, 7 July 2005 is a date remembered by many, and with some discomfort, but on the day that atrocities brought London to its knees, Janeiro Tucker smashed an 88-ball 132 as Bermuda marched to a 113-run victory. It is a significant milestone in Bermudan cricket.

Defeat in the semi-final against eventual champions Scotland may have been disappointing, as was their third-place play-off loss to Canada, but Bermuda left the shores of the Emerald Isle in the knowledge that they could plan ahead for their first appearance in cricket's biggest tournament.

Then, in September 2005, they pulled off a coup: Gus Logie, the former West Indies coach, put pen to paper and agreed a short-term contract (he has since signed an extension) to coach the Bermuda national team.

But controversy hit Bermudan cricket in the first weeks of Logie's reign when, playing in

the Club Match – the showpiece of Bermuda's domestic season – all-rounder Saleem Mukuddem alleged that Herbie Bascome – newly appointed by Logie to the role of assistant national coach – had hurled racial abuse at him.

The spectre of racial abuse loomed large when Bermuda played Namibia in November 2005. In the 36th over of Bermuda's reply (they were on 186 for 7 chasing 388) and after a couple of short balls at their No. 10, Gus Logie pulled his players from the field, claiming that his side had been subjected to a barrage of short deliveries and a volley of verbal abuse. The umpires awarded the game to Namibia; reaction to the incident back in Bermuda was mixed.

Qualification for the World Cup should have heralded a brand-new age for Bermudan cricket, yet here they were, blighted by racial sledging and hampered in their preparation for their biggest competition by ICC regulations. Each of the ICC qualifiers were granted one-day international status through to 2009 to help them in their progress; unfortunately for Bermuda, none of their grounds reach the ICC's requisite standard.

Forced to play their first ever one-day

international, against Canada, in Trinidad, Bermuda put any problems behind them to become only the fourth nation in ODI history to win their first game. They were brought back to earth with a bump, suffering two heavy defeats to Zimbabwe. Two subsequent victories against Canada in Toronto (with Irvine Romaine hitting a century in the second match) boosted morale.

Bermuda will continue their pre-World Cup warm-up by taking part in tri-nations series in the West Indies and South Africa as well as a three-match series against Kenya. They will be boosted by the arrival of Glamorgan batsman David Hemp to their line-up – the former England A player has recently completed the period of qualification to represent the country of his birth…

Bermuda will take their place in their first World Cup finals with their heads held high and you can be sure of one thing: regardless of the results, they will enjoy themselves.

## TOP FIVE PERFORMERS

- **David Hemp**, Glamorgan; LHB; Born: 8 November 1970
- **Janeiro Tucker**, Bermuda; RHB, RAM; Born: 15 March 1975
- **Saleem Mukuddem**, Bermuda; RHB, RAM; Born: 20 January 1972
- **Dean Minors**, Bermuda; LHB, WK; Born: 6 January 1970
- **Dwayne Leverock**, Bermuda; RHB, SLA; Born: 14 July 1971

# NEW ZEALAND

**Black Caps are the Dark Horses**

**New Zealand may remain inconsistent on the Test match circuit but, as many teams have found to their cost, they are a considerable force in the one-day arena and could be the surprise package of the tournament.**

Although New Zealand were granted Test status way back in 1930, they had to wait 26 years before they could celebrate their first victory. When they bowled out the West Indies for 77 on 13 March 1956 to win the final Test by 190 runs, a nation had cause to celebrate. But whereas New Zealand may have struggled in the Test arena, they have always found the one-day format of the game much more to their liking.

**Record breaker:** New Zealand's most capped player, Stephen Fleming is also his country's longest-serving and most successful captain; he can bat a bit, too.

They were the surprise package at the first ever World Cup, in England in 1975, as they made their way to the semi-finals, but their journey came to an end when they slipped to 158 all out and a five-wicket defeat against the West Indies. Still, New Zealand returned home with their heads held high.

Victories over Sri Lanka and India saw them reach the last four when the World Cup returned to England in 1979. This time they faced the hosts at Old Trafford, but they ran out of steam and fell short of the victory target by nine runs.

So when they failed to get beyond the group stages in 1983 their tournament was deemed a failure and two solitary wins against Zimbabwe in the subcontinent four years later, and an early tournament exit, barely lifted the gloom. A side containing Richard Hadlee and Martin Crowe should have done better.

New Zealand's success-starved fans were given something to cheer about when the World Cup came to town in 1992. An opening 37-run win against Australia raised spirits, with Crowe hitting an unbeaten century. New Zealand were employing off-spinner Dipak Patel in an attempt to curb the opening batsmen's initial assault, and the ploy seemed to be working. Sri Lanka were

## FORM GUIDE – Last 50 ODIs

| | |
|---|---|
| Won: | 29 |
| Lost: | 18 |
| Tied: | 0 |
| No result: | 3 |
| Winning percentage: | 61% |
| Highest score: | 397 (v. Zimbabwe, Bulawayo, 24 August 2005) |
| Lowest score: | 105 (v. Australia, Auckland, 3 December 2005) |
| Most runs conceded: | 347 (v. Australia, Napier, 5 March 2005) |
| Runs scored per 6 balls: | 5.11 |
| Runs conceded per 6 balls: | 4.81 |

## TOP FIVE PERFORMERS

- **Nathan Astle**, Canterbury; RHB, RAM; Born: 15 September 1971
- **Shane Bond**, Canterbury; RHB, RAF; Born: 7 June 1975
- **Stephen Fleming**, Canterbury; LHB, captain; Born: 1 April 1973
- **Daniel Vettori**, Northern Districts; LHB, SLA; Born: 27 January 1979
- **Lou Vincent**, Auckland; RHB; Born: 11 November 1978

the next to fall and five further victories followed until the Kiwis crumbled to a Wasim Akram-inspired Pakistan in their final group game in what turned out to be a dress rehearsal for the semi-finals.

And Pakistan did not put a foot wrong when it mattered, either. They reached New Zealand's total of 262 with an over and four wickets to spare. New Zealand were left to ponder what might have been.

They were left scratching their heads four years later following their quarter-final defeat to Australia. Having amassed a challenging 286, Chris Harris impressing with 130, they could only watch in awe as Mark Waugh led from the top of the order, hitting 110 as the Aussies coasted to victory.

They looked impressive in England in 1999, marching to the semi-finals, having beaten Australia along the way. But, just as had been the case seven years earlier, Pakistan proved too strong for them as they coasted to a nine-wicket victory. The 2003 World Cup in South Africa turned out to be a major disappointment they failed to get beyond the Super Six stage.

## SCOTT STYRIS

**Born:** 10 July 1975, Brisbane, Australia
**Debut:** v. India, Rajkot, 5 November 1999

**Clubs:** Auckland, Northern Districts, Middlesex
**Role:** Right-hand batsman, right-arm medium-fast bowler

### ODI STATISTICS

**Batting**

| Mat | inns | no | runs | hs | ave | sr | 100 | 50 | 4s | 6s | ct | st |
|-----|------|-----|------|-----|-------|-------|-----|-----|-----|-----|-----|-----|
| 118 | 101 | 12 | 2592 | 141 | 29.12 | 77.86 | 3 | 15 | 196 | 45 | 45 | 0 |

**Bowling**

| Mat | balls | runs | wkts | bb | ave | econ | sr | 4w | 5w |
|-----|-------|------|------|------|-------|------|-------|-----|-----|
| 118 | 4287 | 3365 | 106 | 6/25 | 31.74 | 4.70 | 40.44 | 3 | 1 |

Having made his one-day international debut in 1999, Styris was forced to wait until 2002 before gaining selection to the Test team – and even then he had to wait a further two months after a bomb in Karachi led to the cancellation of what would have been his debut Test. When his chance finally arrived against the West Indies at St George, he grabbed it with both hands, scoring a century and a half-century. Later that same tour he took 6 for 25 in the one-day series – the best ever one-day figures by a New Zealander. The all-rounder has not looked back since.

The current generation of Black Caps – they adopted the name in 1998 after their sponsors held a competition to choose a new name for the national side – crave success; they are tired of having to live under the shadow of the formidable All Black rugby team, and their results post-South Africa will give New Zealand's cricket fans cause for hope.

Any post-World Cup gloom was lifted when they triumphed in a tri-nations tournament in Pakistan, beating the hosts in the final. But they weren't so happy when they travelled to India for another tri-nations tournament, this time including Australia. The Black Caps won only one of their games and failed to get beyond the group stage. A month later they suffered a 5–0 whitewash in Pakistan.

They turned things around when Pakistan came to New Zealand in January 2004. Captain Stephen Fleming led from the front, finishing with 248 runs in the series, as the home side ran out 4–1 winners. And, following a 5–1 series win against South Africa, they arrived in England later in the year for the ICC Champions Trophy in good heart. But defeat to Australia in the autumn gloom ended any hopes of victory.

Australia were ungracious guests in March 2005, hammering New Zealand 5–0, but confidence was restored later in the year when the Black Caps won a tri-nations tournament in Zimbabwe. Nathan Astle shone in the final, hitting an unbeaten 115 as India were put to the sword.

The progress came to a halt as they slumped to a 4–0 defeat to South Africa, with only opening batsman Lou Vincent emerging from the series with his reputation enhanced. However, encouraging performances in the lead-up to the World Cup, including an excellent victory over Australia in Christchurch – with Scott Styris's swashbuckling 101 the highlight of New Zealand's impressive chase to 332 – and series wins over Sri Lanka and the West Indies (both 4–1), see New Zealand enter the World Cup in a rich vein of form. They are a settled, powerful unit who are capable of embarrassing anyone on their day.

## JOHN BRACEWELL

A tall off-spinner who played 41 Tests and 53 one-day internationals for his country, John Bracewell made his name as coach of Gloucestershire, leading the English county to a string of one-day successes at the turn of the century. He became the New Zealand coach in September 2003.

## WORLD CUP RECORD

| | | | |
|-----|----------------|-----|----------------|
| 1975 | semi-finals | 1992 | semi-finals |
| 1979 | semi-finals | 1996 | quarter-finals |
| 1983 | group stages | 1999 | semi-finals |
| 1987 | group stages | 2003 | Super Six |

# ENGLAND

## GROUP C
### The World Cup's Nearly Men

**All the ingredients that have taken England from Test also-rans to one of the game's most powerful units have deserted them when it comes to one-day cricket. They will travel to the Caribbean woefully short of one-day form.**

Hit by injuries, inconsistent selection and an embarrassing string of defeats, a look in the World Cup history books will give England fans little comfort: they have endured nothing but World Cup disappointment.

Hosting the first three events, they set a precedent – some might call it a curse – that is still

**England's talisman:** Where Freddie treads, his country tends to follow. Strong, aggressive and exceptionally talented, Andrew Flintoff has developed into the world's best all-rounder.

to be broken: no nation has ever lifted the World Cup in their own country.

They got off to a good start in 1975, sailing through their group unbeaten to face Australia in the semi-final, where they slumped to 93 all out. Australia reached the target with four overs to spare.

A nation dared to dream as England made it to the final four years later, but the West Indies had other ideas. Chasing 287 for victory, England slipped to 194 all out.

More disappointment followed in 1983. Strong favourites to beat India in the semi-final at Old Trafford, the underdogs came good and cruised to a six-wicket victory.

England finally appeared to be shaking any past World Cup gloom from their shoulders when they travelled to the subcontinent in 1987. Four wins and two defeats were enough to secure them a place in the semi-final against India in Bombay, where a magnificent 115 from Graham Gooch secured them a 35-run win.

And with England cruising on 135 for 2, chasing Australia's 253, it seemed they would finally get their hands on cricket's most coveted trophy. But then Mike Gatting tried to reverse-sweep Allan Border; he got a top edge and was caught behind. Their captain's downfall triggered a collapse from which they never recovered. It was an opportunity lost.

They had a chance to make up for it four years later, and a combination of rain clouds and an illogical run-rate law saw them defeat South Africa

### WORLD CUP RECORD

| | | | |
|---|---|---|---|
| 1975 | semi-finals | 1992 | runners-up |
| 1979 | runners-up | 1996 | quarter-finals |
| 1983 | semi-finals | 1999 | Super Six |
| 1987 | runners-up | 2003 | group stages |

### DUNCAN FLETCHER

The former Zimbabwe captain – he led his side to a famous victory over Australia in the 1983 World Cup – had instant coaching success with both Western Province and Glamorgan. England came calling and, in 1999, he became the first foreigner to coach the national side and has transformed their fortunes.

in the semi-final to give themselves another shot at the title. However, with England chasing 250 for victory, the Pakistan bowlers, led by Wasim Akram and Mushtaq Ahmed, revelled under the Melbourne lights and England fell 22 runs short.

The host's curse struck in 1999 and England crashed out of the tournament at the group stages, but their departure from South Africa 2003 at the same stage led to widespread sympathy.

As the tournament approached against the backdrop of political unrest in Zimbabwe, England became the pawns in what was fast becoming a political nightmare. The players decided to forfeit the game. Defeats to India and Australia did not help, but the players' decision to stand up for what they thought was right had cost

## KEVIN PIETERSEN

**Born:** 27 June 1980, Pietermaritzburg, South Africa
**Debut:** v. Zimbabwe, Harare, 28 November 2004

**Clubs:** Natal, Nottinghamshire
**Role:** Right-hand batsman, right-arm off-break bowler

### ODI STATISTICS

| Mat | inns | no | runs | hs | Batting ave | sr | 100 | 50 | 4s | 6s | ct | st |
|---|---|---|---|---|---|---|---|---|---|---|---|---|
| 41 | 35 | 8 | 1500 | 116 | 55.55 | 95.17 | 3 | 10 | 151 | 35 | 20 | 0 |

| Mat | balls | runs | wkts | bb | Bowling ave | econ | sr | 4w | 5w |
|---|---|---|---|---|---|---|---|---|---|
| 41 | 84 | 91 | 1 | 1/4 | 91.00 | 6.50 | 84.00 | 0 | 0 |

Kevin Pietersen translates his swaggering on-the-field manner into the way he plays the game and he made a sensational start to his international career. In just his second one-day series, playing against the country of his birth in South Africa, he scored 434 runs in seven innings (av. 151.33) with three centuries. He took his cavalier one-day form into the Test arena and won the hearts of a nation when his 158 at The Oval in September 2005 secured the Ashes. He may not be to everybody's taste, but Kevin Pietersen has taken the art of batsmanship to an entirely new level and his form will be crucial to England's World Cup hopes.

them a shot at the game's biggest prize.

The débâcle of South Africa heralded the start of a new era for English cricket. Michael Vaughan took over the captaincy; Andrew Flintoff started to establish himself as the game's finest all-rounder and, when England returned to Africa in the winter of 2004, they introduced an African jewel of their own to the international cricket audience.

England may have lost the series 4–1, but the result was the last thing on people's lips. New boy Kevin Pietersen scored 454 runs at an average of 151.33 and had hit three centuries along the way. England had unearthed a diamond.

They started to get back to winning ways in the one-day series that preceded the start of their famous Ashes win, reaching the NatWest Series final against Australia; the game was a thriller, ending in a tie. And they were competitive in the pre-Ashes money-spinner, the NatWest Challenge against Australia, despite going down 2–1.

But cracks in the England machine first started to appear in the subcontinent the winter following

their Ashes triumph. Without captain Vaughan and paceman Simon Jones, England slid to a 3–2 series defeat in Pakistan.

Worse was to follow. Shorn of Marcus Trescothick at the top of the order and Stephen Harmison with the new ball, an experimental England were found wanting against India. Only a stubborn innings of 74 from Andrew Strauss in the sixth one-day international in Jahshedpur prevented a series whitewash.

But that is exactly what they suffered against Sri Lanka back in England the following summer, with Andrew Flintoff this time taking his place in sickbay. An experimental England side then took some credit from a drawn series with Pakistan.

For England to win in the Caribbean, their big-name players will have to be fit and firing on all cylinders. However, with the World Cup coming off the back of what will have been a massive Ashes campaign, the chances of that happening are on a par with the bookies' current rating of England's tournament chances … very slim indeed.

# KENYA GROUP C
### Test Nation in Waiting

**Following their march to the semi-finals in the 2003 World Cup, it seemed only a matter of time before Kenya became the 11th Test nation, but then Kenyan cricket was rocked by a series of controversies.**

First the spectre of match-fixing reared its ugly head and, after being investigated and found guilty of receiving money from a bookmaker, former captain Maurice Odumbe was banned for five years, a ban that effectively ends his cricket career.

Then, in January 2005, the Kenyan Minister of Sports, Ochillo Ayacko, fired Kenya Cricket Association chairman Sharad Ghai and his entire executive committee amid accusations of failing to account for sponsorship money and for having operated illegally for seven years. In an attempt to put an end to the corruption, a new cricket body, Cricket Kenya, was formed.

Even that conciliatory move had repercussions. In June 2005, Kenya were stripped of their one-

day international status, a ruling that will come into force for the 2009 ICC Trophy: for Kenya to regain their former status, they will have to finish in the tournament's top six. After the highs of South Africa, it was a crashing fall to earth.

Their World Cup journey began at the inaugural competition in 1975 when, along with players from Uganda and Tanzania, they made up a side to represent East Africa. However, three heavy defeats led to an early exit and the experiment was not repeated at future World Cups.

It came as little surprise when Kenya broke away from their East African triumvirate and joined the ICC as an associate member in their own right in 1981. The following year, they entered their first tournament as a nation – the 1982 ICC Trophy in England. They won three and lost two of their games and exited the tournament at the group stages. It was a similar story when the tournament returned to England four years later.

The tournament's switch from England to the Netherlands in 1990 seemed to suit Kenya down to the ground and they made it through to the semi-finals where they faced the hosts. However, they were blown away by the medium-pace bowling of PJ Bakker, who took 6 for 41, to reach a disappointing total of 202. The Netherlands cruised to the target with four overs to spare and Kenyan dreams were dashed for another year.

Expectations were high as Kenya played host to the tournament four years later. They did not disappoint, marching through their initial

## ROGER HARPER

A tall off-spinner who played 25 Tests and 105 one-day internationals for the West Indies, Roger Harper was one of the finest fielders the game has ever seen. He was coach of the West Indies between 2000 and 2003, in what were uncertain times in Caribbean cricket. He was appointed Kenya coach in January 2006.

**Kenya's linchpin:** Dubbed the "Black Botham" early in his career, Thomas Odoyo is the only Kenyan to have scored 1,000 runs and taken 50 wickets in one-day internationals.

group stages unbeaten to take their place in the semi-finals. For a nation that had had little to cheer about in cricket terms, their 64-run win over Bermuda – with Maurice Odumbe scoring a magnificent 158 not out – was a cause for national celebration.

They had made it through to the last hurrah of their own party but, more significantly, the

## STEVE TIKOLO

**Born:** 25 June 1971, Nairobi, Kenya
**Debut:** v. India, Cuttack, 18 February 1996

**Clubs:** Kenya, Border
**Role:** Right-hand batsman, right-arm medium bowler

### ODI STATISTICS

**Batting**

| Mat | inns | no | runs | hs | ave | sr | 100 | 50 | ct | st |
|---|---|---|---|---|---|---|---|---|---|---|
| 79 | 77 | 3 | 2124 | 106* | 28.70 | 74.08 | 1 | 17 | 32 | 0 |

**Bowling**

| Mat | balls | runs | wkts | bb | ave | econ | sr | 4w | 5w |
|---|---|---|---|---|---|---|---|---|---|
| 79 | 2118 | 1728 | 50 | 3/14 | 34.56 | 4.89 | 42.36 | 0 | 0 |

Steve Tikolo is the best cricketer Kenya has ever produced. He played in Kenya's first ever one-day international, against Sri Lanka in the 1996 World Cup, and marked the occasion by scoring 65. He then booked Kenya's place at the next World Cup with a brutal 147 against Bangladesh in the ICC Trophy final. His finest moments came when he masterminded his country's unexpected march to the semi-finals in South Africa in 2003. Tikolo gave up the captaincy in 2004 to concentrate on his batting and West Indies 2007 will be a fitting stage for the African who has just a touch of Caribbean flair about his game.

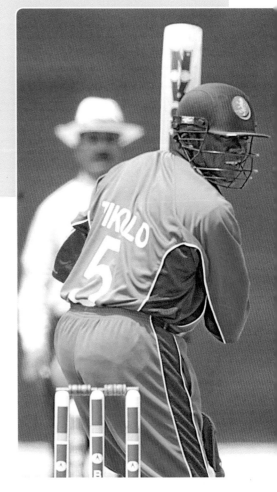

victory had ensured Kenya's qualification for the 1996 World Cup; if you were looking for the most significant win in Kenyan cricket history to date, look no further. A two-wicket defeat to the UAE in the final may have come as some disappointment, but the majority of Kenyans now had larger cricket venues to dream about.

Three opening defeats may have shattered any lofty ambitions, but a victory over the once-mighty West Indies sent shockwaves around the cricket world and led to mass celebrations in the streets of Nairobi. Few would have thought that Kenya's 166 all out could have posed any problems for the powerful Caribbean batting line-up, but spells of 3 for 17 from Rajab Ali and 3 for 15 from Maurice Odumbe sent the West Indies spiralling to an embarrassing 93 all out. Kenya had 11 new sporting heroes; a 144-run defeat in their final game mattered little – months after the World Cup, Kenya were granted one-day status, their first significant step up cricket's ladder.

However, if Kenya's newfound position was supposed to lead to a marked improvement in

their cricket fortunes, five straight World Cup defeats in England in 1999 showed there was still marked room for improvement.

All of which made their progress through the 2003 World Cup all the more extraordinary. They may have been helped by circumstances beyond the boundary rope – New Zealand refused to play in Nairobi for security reasons and Kenya were awarded the match – but victories over Sri Lanka by 51 runs in the group stages (with Collins Obuya taking 5 for 24) and a comfortable seven-wicket win over Zimbabwe in the Super Six stage, meant that Kenya had earned their shock semi-final place on merit. That they proved no match for India in the biggest game in their cricket history was of no consequence. Cricket in Kenya had come a long way.

However, heavy defeats in a tournament in Sharjah and an early exit from the ICC Champions Trophy in England in September 2004 preceded a period of unprecedented turmoil in Kenyan cricket. As a result, it was another 18 months before they played another one-day international.

A 2–2 series draw in Zimbabwe, with fast

bowler Peter Ongondo impressing with the ball, was followed by a 4–0 whitewash in Bangladesh. Victories over Canada in Toronto followed, before Bangladesh came to town and handed out another cricket lesson.

Further pre-World Cup warm-up games against the likes of Bermuda will do much to restore confidence, but when they step off the plane in the Caribbean, it will be a major surprise if Kenya repeat their feats of 2003.

# CANADA

## GROUP C
### Juniors of World Cricket

**Canada showed a considerable fighting spirit in South Africa in 2003, recording a surprise win against Bangladesh along the way and, having qualified for their second successive World Cup, they will be looking for a repeat performance in the Caribbean.**

Just as the game had spread through other member states of the Commonwealth, so it found a home in Canada. Indeed, when Canada played the United States in an international match in 1844, they competed in what is considered the oldest international fixture in sport, not just cricket; the match took place some 30 years before the first Ashes fixture. By 1867, the game was considered so popular it was named Canada's national sport.

However, over the course of the next century, as the popularity of baseball in the United States escalated and spread north of the border, cricket in Canada started its own gradual decline. Be that as it may, there still remained enough of an

**Match-winner:** Austin Codrington's 5 for 37 led Canada to a shock win over Bangladesh at the last World Cup. The fast-medium bowler and hard-hitting lower-order batsman will be hoping to repeat the trick in 2007.

interest for them to take their place proudly in the first ICC Trophy, staged in England in 1979.

With the three group winners and the best runner-up making up the quartet for the semi-finals, Canada, who finished second in their group, might have considered themselves fortunate to be in the last four. But they beat Bermuda convincingly to reach the final. And, although they were beaten comprehensively by Sri Lanka, Canada had achieved their pre-tournament mission: qualification for the 1979 World Cup.

It did not turn out to be the most memorable of occasions for Canada. Following defeats to Pakistan (by eight wickets), England (by eight

### WORLD CUP RECORD

| | |
|---|---|
| **1979** group stages | **2003** group stages |

wickets, with Canada having been bowled out for a paltry 44) and Australia (by seven wickets), Canada left for home having made little mark on the tournament. It would be another 24 years before they could take part again on the world's biggest cricket stage.

In between times they tested themselves in the ICC Trophy. Their return to England in 1983 was blighted by rain, and three washouts did not help their quest; they crashed out of the tournament after the group stages. The sun may have been shining on England four years later, but Canada lost three of their group games – including a painful 72-run reverse to arch-rivals, the United States – to fall at the first hurdle once again.

A switch to the Netherlands in 1990 did little to change their fortunes and Canada failed to get beyond the second group stage; having beaten the hosts in the opening game of phase

## JOHN DAVISON

**Born:** 9 May 1970, Vancouver Island, Canada  
**Debut:** v. Bangladesh, Durban, 11 February 2003

**Clubs:** Canada, South Australia, Victoria  
**Role:** Right-hand batsman, right-arm off-break bowler

### ODI STATISTICS

**Batting**

| Mat | inns | no | runs | hs | ave | sr | 100 | 50 | 4s | 6s | ct | st |
|-----|------|-----|------|-----|-------|--------|-----|-----|-----|-----|-----|-----|
| 12 | 12 | 0 | 323 | 111 | 26.91 | 107.66 | 1 | 2 | 33 | 13 | 4 | 0 |

**Bowling**

| Mat | balls | runs | wkts | bb | ave | econ | sr | 4w | 5w |
|-----|-------|------|------|------|-------|------|-------|-----|-----|
| 12 | 558 | 395 | 19 | 3/15 | 20.78 | 4.24 | 29.36 | 0 | 0 |

A pinch-hitting opener and an off-spinner of some renown, John Davison is Canada's most experienced player and, by some distance, its best. Having failed to secure a place in the Victoria side, from 1999 he took up various coaching posts in North America and was soon included in Canada's representative side. He played his part in securing Canada's berth in the 2003 World Cup where he became the tournament's unlikely star, hitting the World Cup's fastest ever century against the West Indies and ending as Canada's leading run-scorer and wicket-taker. He cemented his reputation as a quality all-rounder when he took 17 for 137 in Canada's first-class match against the USA and scored 84 as Canada won by 104 runs.

## TOP FIVE PERFORMERS

- **Sanjayan Thuraisingam**, Canada; RHB, RAFM;  
  Born: 11 September 1969
- **Umar Bhatti**, Canada; LHB, LAM;  
  Born: 4 January 1984
- **Kevin Sandher**, Canada; RHB, SLA;  
  Born: 16 July 1980
- **Henry Osinde**, Canada; RHB, RAMF;  
  Born: 17 October 1978
- **Austin Codrington**, Canada; RHB, RAMF;  
  Born: 22 August 1975

two, they slid to two defeats – against Denmark and Bangladesh – and found themselves at the bottom of the table.

They fell in phase two when the tournament moved to Kenya in 1994 and again in Malaysia four years later. These were infuriating times for Canadian cricket fans.

There's nothing like hosting a tournament to get the fans' pulses racing and, with Toronto the host city for the 2001 ICC Trophy, Canada's players responded in style. Their progress through the group stages could hardly be described as comfortable, but it still left Canada in contention for one of the three coveted places for the 2003 World Cup in South Africa.

All good dramas need a twist; Canada's came when they finished fourth in the Super League stage to earn a one-off, winner-takes-all showdown with Scotland for the final World Cup berth. A nation held its breath.

Played two days after the ICC Trophy final (won by the Netherlands), you could have cut the tension with a knife. Canada, inspired by 5 for 25 by Sanjayan Thuraisingam, managed to restrict

## FORM GUIDE – Last 15 ODIs

| | |
|---|---|
| Played: | 15 |
| Won: | 1 |
| Lost: | 14 |
| Tied: | 0 |
| No result: | 0 |
| Winning percentage: | 7% |
| Highest score: | 261 (v. Bermuda, Toronto, 21 August 2006) |
| Lowest score: | 36 (v. Sri Lanka, Paarl, 19 February 2003) |
| Most runs conceded: | 272 (v. Bermuda, Toronto, 21 August 2006) |
| Runs scored per 6 balls: | 3.33 |
| Runs conceded per 6 balls: | 4.67 |

Scotland to 176 for 9; Canada cruised to the target with ten overs to spare; so much for tension.

And, to the surprise of many, they started their World Cup campaign with a victory, by 60 runs against Bangladesh, with Austin Codrington taking 5 for 27. A narrow defeat to Kenya was followed by embarrassment: bowled out for 36 against Sri Lanka. Canada went down fighting against the West Indies, though, with John Davison hitting the tournament's fastest ever century (off just 67 balls), but they posed few problems for either New Zealand or South Africa. Canada may have fallen at the first hurdle, but they had shown significant fight.

They showed similar qualities in Ireland in the 2005 ICC Trophy. They may have missed out on a place in the final when they lost to the hosts in the last four, but qualification for the semi-finals had secured their World Cup place in the Caribbean. They cantered to a five-wicket victory over Bermuda to secure third place. It mattered little; Canada had achieved their main objective once again.

But their preparation for the World Cup has been difficult; they have lost to the likes of Zimbabwe, Kenya and, most disappointingly of all, to Bermuda. Their eclectic mix of players will be under no illusions about the difficulty of the task confronting them in the Caribbean. Victories over England and New Zealand will be beyond them, but expect them to put up a hell of a fight in their opening game in St Lucia: that match, against Kenya, will be Canada's World Cup final.

# PAKISTAN GROUP D

**Strong Contenders**

These are troubled times for Pakistan cricket: an abandoned Test match, ball-tampering allegations, an argument with an umpire and two bowling stars failing drugs tests see them as a team under fire. Expect them to come out firing when the tournament begins.

Pakistan's first World Cup appearance in the inaugural tournament in 1975 is one they would prefer to forget. Blown away by Dennis Lillee (5 for 34), they slumped to 205 all out and an opening 73-run defeat to Australia. They had the West Indies on the ropes at 203 for 9, chasing 267 for victory, in their next game, but a 64-run last-wicket stand between Deryck Murray and Andy Roberts saw the Caribbean side to a nervy one-wicket victory. A crushing 192-run win over Sri Lanka saw them bow out of the tournament in style, but it had been a disappointing campaign for Pakistan.

They fared better four years later, cruising past Canada in their opening game and then getting past Australia by 89 runs. They had already qualified for the semi-finals by the time they faced England in their final group game, but a 14-

run defeat did little for morale and, worse, meant that Pakistan would face the West Indies in the semi-finals. The Caribbean outfit proved too strong: Pakistan slipped to a 43-run defeat and a tournament exit.

They squeezed into the semi-finals four years later, pipping New Zealand on run-rate, but the 1983 World Cup will provoke uncomfortable memories for Pakistan cricket fans. They fell once again to the West Indies but, even worse, their arch-rivals, India, went on to shock the Caribbean giants in the final to lift the trophy for the first time.

Expectations were high when Pakistan played host, with India, to the 1987 World Cup. And they were on course to fulfil the expectations of a nation when they faced Australia in the semi-finals in Lahore. They fell to an 18-run defeat and a nation was inconsolable.

An opening ten-wicket defeat to the West Indies did not bode well for Pakistan four years later, but aided by a turnaround in form, and a helping hand from the weather, they scraped through to the semi-finals to face New Zealand. A 37-ball 60 from new boy Inzamam-ul-Haq propelled them into the final against England and there, under the Melbourne lights, Wasim Akram and Mushtaq Ahmed combined to dash England's hopes. An emotional Imran Khan lifted the trophy; it was a fairytale end for Pakistan's inspirational captain.

However, a quarter-final defeat to India when

**Razzler Dazzler:** Abdul Razzaq is a hard-hitting batsman and accurate fast-medium bowler. He is widely recognized as Pakistan's most formidable all-rounder since the legendary Imran Khan.

the tournament returned to the subcontinent in 1996 left Pakistan's cricket fans in uproar. They had a point to prove in England three years later.

They eased their way into the semi-finals, where they would face New Zealand and, inspired by an unbeaten 113 from Saeed Anwar, they cruised through to the final following a comfortable nine-wicket win. Hopes were high.

They were summarily smashed by Australia in the most one-sided final in World Cup history.

## BOB WOOLMER

A former Test batsman for England, Bob Woolmer has a surgically analytical approach to cricket. As such, perhaps it is not surprising that he has tasted more success as a coach than he did as a player, enjoying four successful years with South Africa before taking charge of Pakistan in June 2004.

## WORLD CUP RECORD

| | | | |
|---|---|---|---|
| 1975 | group stages | 1992 | CHAMPIONS |
| 1979 | semi-finals | 1996 | quarter-finals |
| 1983 | semi-finals | 1999 | runners-up |
| 1987 | semi-finals | 2003 | group stages |

Bowled out for 132, they were forced to sit back and watch as Australia raced to the target in just 20.1 overs. Seeking to make amends in South Africa in 2003, they failed to make it through the group stages; another World Cup had ended in bitter disappointment. Things had to change.

A home series against Bangladesh is as good a way as any to restore confidence, and with Inzamam taking over the captaincy from Rashid Latif, they cantered to a 5–0 series whitewash. South Africa were the next visitors to Pakistan, and they would provide an altogether sterner challenge: the series went to the wire, but South Africa came out on top of the decider, winning by seven wickets.

A 5–0 home win over New Zealand indicated that Pakistan's one-day form was back on track, but they wobbled in the return series Down Under, losing 4–1, and then lost 3–2 to India; hardly the best tonic.

When they arrived in England for the ICC Champions Trophy in September 2004, they were

desperately short of form. They made it through to the semi-finals, before coming unstuck against the West Indies, slipping to 131 all out and a seven-wicket defeat.

A crushing defeat to Sri Lanka in the Paktel Cup final in October 2004 was followed by a six-wicket win over India. They headed to Australia for the VB Series with renewed confidence and performed well, making it to the final, only to lose the three-match series 2–0.

Naved-ul-Hasan shone with the ball as Pakistan romped to a much welcome 4–2 win over India and series wins over the West Indies

and England followed. When India came to town at the beginning of 2006, Pakistan finally seemed to have found some consistency. They came unstuck against their biggest rivals, losing 4–1. Series wins over Sri Lanka, followed by a drawn series with England, would have done much to restore confidence.

You can never write off a side like Pakistan. By the time they arrive in the West Indies, the dust will have settled on the ball-tampering debate; these allegations hurt the Pakistan team and they will no doubt feel as though they have plenty to prove come the 2007 World Cup.

## MOHAMMAD YOUSUF

**Born:** 27 August 1974, Lahore, Pakistan
**Debut:** v. Zimbabwe, Harare, 28 March 1998

**Clubs:** Bahawalpur, Lahore
**Role:** Right-hand batsman

### ODI STATISTICS

| Mat | inns | no | runs | hs | ave | sr | 100 | 50 | 4s | 6s | ct | st |
|---|---|---|---|---|---|---|---|---|---|---|---|---|
| 226 | 214 | 30 | 7580 | 141* | 41.19 | 74.07 | 11 | 51 | 607 | 78 | 50 | 0 |

### Bowling

| Mat | balls | runs | wkts | bb | ave | econ | sr | 4w | 5w |
|---|---|---|---|---|---|---|---|---|---|
| 226 | 1 | 1 | 0 | - | - | - | 6.00 | 0 | 0 |

Formerly known as Yousuf Youhana, until his recent conversion to Islam, Muhammad Yousuf was only one of a handful of Christians to have played for Pakistan. After a difficult debut against South Africa in 1998, he sprang to the public's attention a year later with an unbeaten 120 v. Zimbabwe at Lahore and was one of the few Pakistan players to emerge with any credit after Zimbabwe's shock series win. The runs continued to flow for Yousuf and he has become a vital member of Pakistan's world-class middle-order. Averaging 53.12 in the Test arena, he is equally adept in the one-day format of the game.

# WEST INDIES GROUP D
### The Hosts are Hungry for Success

**There was a time when the West Indies made the World Cup their very own and, with the tournament arriving in the Caribbean for the first time, their fans will be hoping for a return to the halcyon days.**

The inaugural World Cup provided the perfect stage for a talented West Indies team to show their skills to not only their own cricket-mad fans but also to the wider global audience, and their march through the tournament was as intimidating as it was impressive. They swatted Sri Lanka aside in their opening game, strolling to a nine-wicket victory.

They were made to work harder by Pakistan in the next match. Chasing 267 for victory, they slid to 99 for 5, but recovered and limped to a

### WORLD CUP RECORD

| | | | |
|---|---|---|---|
| 1975 | CHAMPIONS | 1992 | group stages |
| 1979 | CHAMPIONS | 1996 | semi-finals |
| 1983 | runners-up | 1999 | group stages |
| 1987 | group stages | 2003 | group stages |

**Trinidad's new treasure:** Capable of turning a match with bat and ball, West Indian cricket has waited a long time for all-rounder Dwayne Bravo's international emergence.

one-wicket win. With a semi-final place already assured, they then cantered to a comfortable win over Australia.

New Zealand singularly failed to cope with the West Indies' bowlers in the semi-final at The Oval, and their 158 all out total was never going to trouble the Caribbean outfit; the West Indies made it home with 20 overs in hand.

And so to Australia and the final: Lord's had never seen anything like it, with the famous old ground becoming a Caribbean oasis for the day. The team did not disappoint their fans, either. Captain Clive Lloyd smashed an 85-ball 102 as the West Indies reached 291 for 8. Australia, with an astonishing five run outs on their card, fell 17 runs short. The West Indies were now officially the best team in the world.

They never looked like relinquishing their crown when the tournament returned to England four years later. Defeats of India and New Zealand (their fixture with Sri Lanka was washed out) were

### BENNETT KING

A promising junior player whose career was cut short by injury, King became Queensland coach after the position was vacated by John Buchanan's promotion to lead the national team. He led Queensland to Pura Milk Cup success in his first year in charge, 1999–2000, and was appointed West Indies coach in 2004.

enough to take them through to the semi-finals, where they proved too strong for Pakistan.

And with England on 183 for 2 needing 287 for victory, there were times when an upset looked as though it could be on the cards. Joel Garner had other ideas, taking 5 for 38 as England lost their last eight wickets for a paltry 11 runs. West Indies were the world champions once again.

They were strong favourites to complete the hat-trick in 1983. An opening 34-run defeat to India was merely seen as a wobble, particularly when they comfortably won their

## FORM GUIDE – Last 50 ODIs

| | |
|---|---|
| Won: | 22 |
| Lost: | 26 |
| Tied: | 0 |
| No result: | 2 |
| Winning percentage: | 46% |
| Highest score: | 339 (v. Pakistan, Adelaide, 28 January 2005) |
| Lowest score: | 80 (v. Sri Lanka, Mumbai, 14 October 2006) |
| Most runs conceded: | 324 (v. New Zealand, Napier, 1 March 2006) |
| Runs scored per 6 balls: | 4.86 |
| Runs conceded per 6 balls: | 4.90 |

## BRIAN LARA

**Born:** 2 May 1969, Cantaro, Santa Cruz, Trinidad
**Debut:** v. Pakistan, Karachi, 9 November 1990

**Clubs:** Trinidad & Tobago, Warwickshire, Northern Transvaal
**Role:** Left-hand batsman

### ODI STATISTICS

| | | | | | Batting | | | | | | | |
|---|---|---|---|---|---|---|---|---|---|---|---|---|
| Mat | inns | no | runs | hs | ave | sr | 100 | 50 | 4s | 6s | ct | st |
| 283 | 274 | 30 | 9948 | 169 | 40.77 | 79.34 | 19 | 61 | 1000 | 123 | 114 | 0 |

| | | | | Bowling | | | | |
|---|---|---|---|---|---|---|---|---|
| Mat | balls | runs | wkts | bb | ave | econ | sr | 4w | 5w |
| 283 | 49 | 61 | 4 | 2/5 | 15.25 | 7.46 | 12.25 | 0 | 0 |

In the space of two months in 1994, Brian Lara went on a spree of run scoring that saw him break the record score in both Test (375) and first-class cricket (501 not out). Several unproductive spells as West Indies captain followed, but the runs continued to flow: he put Australia to the sword in 1998–99 with a scoring sequence of 213, 8, 153 not out and 100 and, three years later, scored 688 runs in a three-Test series against Sri Lanka. He cemented his legend when he regained the Test record from Matthew Hayden in April 2004 and has since gone on to beat Allan Border's record Test tally of runs.

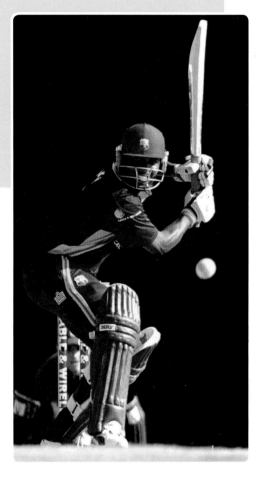

remaining group games before brushing aside the attentions of Pakistan in the semi-finals. The final provided the West Indies with an opportunity to exact revenge: India would challenge them for the game's biggest prize.

However, when India slid to 183 all out, the kettledrums and horns were blaring once again. India duly silenced them, as a stunned West Indies slid to 140 all out and a 43-run defeat.

The slide had started. Three victories in the subcontinent in 1987 were accompanied by three defeats, and the once Caribbean kings failed to make it through the group stages. A similar fate befell them in Australia and New Zealand four years later.

They scraped through the group stages in 1996 – despite suffering the ignominy of a 73-run defeat to Kenya – and a 19-run victory over South Africa in the quarter-finals, with Brian Lara hitting a superb 111, suggested a return to the glory days.

And when they were cruising along on 165 for 2, requiring 208 for victory, they seemed destined

for another appearance in the final. They lost their last eight wickets for 37 runs and slumped to a demoralizing defeat. They suffered an early exit in both 1999 and 2003.

It wasn't all bad news. In September 2004, on the back of a crushing Test series defeat to England, the West Indies took their place in the ICC Champions Trophy short of both form and confidence. Successive victories over Bangladesh, South Africa and Pakistan handed them a place in the final against England. Chasing 218 for victory, they slipped to 147 for 8 in the Oval gloom, but an unbroken ninth-wicket stand of 71 between Courtney Browne and Ian Bradshaw handed them both the trophy and their brightest day in cricket for 20 years.

They failed to continue the momentum: failure to reach the VB Series final in Australia was a disappointment; a 5–0 whitewash to South Africa was a calamity. Another whitewash followed, this time to Pakistan, and following a 4–1 defeat to New Zealand, it was clear something had to change.

The West Indies turned to Brian Lara for inspiration and the talismanic left-hander took over the captaincy reins once again. Zimbabwe

may not provide the toughest opposition these days, but a 5–0 series win showed a marked improvement. When they went on to beat India 4–1, it seemed as though the tide had finally turned and their march to the final of the 2006 ICC Champions Trophy showed how much they have improved.

No nation has ever lifted the World Cup on its own soil and despite a recent upturn in fortune it would still be a major surprise if the West Indies were to reverse that trend.

## TOP PERFORMERS

- **Dwayne Bravo,** Trinidad & Tobago; RHB, RAMF; Born: 7 October 1983
- **Shivnarine Chanderpaul,** Guyana; LHB, LS; Born: 16 August 1974
- **Fidel Edwards,** Barbados; RHB, RAF; Born: 6 February 1982
- **Chris Gayle,** Jamaica; RHB, OS; Born: 21 September 1979
- **Ramnaresh Sarwan,** Guyana; RHB, LS; Born: 23 June 1980

# ZIMBABWE

Team in Turmoil

**For those who think politics and sport should not mix, there is no finer example of how a nation's sporting hopes can be decimated by a political regime than Zimbabwe. As Robert Mugabe's regime tightens its grip, so Zimbabwe's cricket stock continues to fall.**

Against the backdrop of troubled times in their own country, two of Zimbabwe's most celebrated players, Andy Flower and Henry Olonga, took to the field during the 2003 World Cup wearing black armbands to mark the "death of democracy" in their country. It effectively marked the end of their international careers – Olonga was even forced to live in exile – and led to a string of unprecedented events in world cricket.

The following year it was announced that captain Heath Streak had resigned the captaincy and retired from international cricket. Over the course of the next few days, it emerged that the choice was anything but voluntary: he had been forced to leave the post.

His fellow white players submitted a list to Zimbabwe Cricket, the game's governing body, demanding the reinstatement of their captain and a review of the team's selection process, hoping to eliminate the political and racial bias that had been imposed on the national team by Robert Mugabe's government.

The demands were ignored, the players were jettisoned from the squad and it heralded a "new" era for Zimbabwe cricket. A young and inexperienced squad were then comprehensively trounced by Sri Lanka. It brought all of the progress Zimbabwe had made in world cricket over the previous decade to a bitter end.

Zimbabwe's climb up world cricket's ladder had been slow. Having missed out on the first two World Cups, they took their place in the 1983 tournament with little international experience.

## WORLD CUP RECORD

| | | | |
|---|---|---|---|
| 1983 | group stages | 1996 | group stages |
| 1987 | group stages | 1999 | Super Six |
| 1992 | group stages | 2003 | Super Six |

## KEVIN CURRAN

A fiery character who enjoyed a successful county career with Gloucestershire and Northamptonshire, and who played for Zimbabwe in two World Cups, Kevin Curran was Zimbabwe's assistant coach before taking over the reins with Namibia. He returned to Zimbabwe as director of the Harare cricket academy and replaced Phil Simmons as national coach in August 2005.

But their first taste of World Cup cricket was one of sweet success. Led by Duncan Fletcher, now England's cricket supremo and the man responsible for the turnaround in that nation's fortunes, they stunned Australia at Trent Bridge to win by 13 runs. That was as good as it got, but Zimbabwe left England with their heads held high.

They looked set for a win in their opening game against New Zealand in the subcontinent four years later. Chasing 243 for victory, Dave Houghton smashed a magnificent 142, but his fall signalled an end to Zimbabwe's chances and they fell an agonizing three runs short. They then fell to five straight defeats.

Seven losses in their first seven games in Australia and New Zealand in 1992 confined them to an early tournament exit yet again, but victory over England in their final match would

have made their long journey home slightly more comfortable. It was the last World Cup Zimbabwe would play as an associate member of the ICC; four months later they were granted Test status – they had joined cricket's elite.

They left the 1996 World Cup without a win to their name, but headed to England three years later with their strongest ever squad and proved the tournament's surprise package. A comfortable opening five-wicket win against Kenya was followed by a nervy three-run victory over India. However, defeats to Sri Lanka and England meant that nothing short of victory over South Africa would do if they wanted to progress further in the tournament.

They did not disappoint. Neil Johnson starred with both bat and ball as Zimbabwe brushed their neighbours aside with a 48-run victory. They had made it beyond the group stages of the World Cup for the first time and, although their win over South Africa was their last, progress was clearly being made.

All of which made the events of 2003 hard to savour for Zimbabwe cricket fans. They made it through to the Super Six stage of the tournament once again, but their performances on the field were overshadowed by political rumblings beyond the boundary rope and most cricket

## TOP FIVE PERFORMERS

- **Terry Duffin**, Midlands; LHB; Born: 20 March 1982
- **Hamilton Masakadza**, Mashonaland; RHB, OS; Born: 9 August 1983
- **Stuart Matsikenyeri**, Manicaland; RHB, OS; Born: 3 May 1983
- **Vusi Sibanda**, Zimbabwe Cricket Academy; RHB; Born: 10 October 1983
- **Prosper Utseya**, Mashonaland; RHB, OD, captain; Born: 26 March 1985

## FORM GUIDE - Last 50 ODIs

| | |
|---|---|
| Won: | 10 |
| Lost: | 39 |
| Tied: | 0 |
| No result: | 1 |
| Winning percentage: | 21% |
| Highest score: | 338 (v. Bermuda, Port of Spain, 18 May 2006) |
| Lowest score: | 65 (v. India, Harare, 29 August 2005) |
| Most runs conceded: | 418 (v. South Africa, Potchefstroom, 20 September 2006) |
| Runs scored per 6 balls: | 4.17 |
| Runs conceded per 6 balls: | 5.12 |

## BRENDAN TAYLOR

**Born:** 6 February 1986, Harare, Zimbabwe  **Club:** Mashonaland A
**Debut:** v. Sri Lanka, Bulawayo, 20 April 2004  **Role:** Right-hand batsman, right-arm off-break bowler, wicket-keeper

### ODI STATISTICS

| | | | | | Batting | | | | | | | |
|---|---|---|---|---|---|---|---|---|---|---|---|---|
| Mat | inns | no | runs | hs | ave | sr | 100 | 50 | 4s | 6s | ct | st |
| 53 | 53 | 5 | 1447 | 98 | 30.14 | 65.38 | 0 | 10 | 136 | 19 | 28 | 9 |

| | | | Bowling | | | | | | |
|---|---|---|---|---|---|---|---|---|---|
| Mat | balls | runs | wkts | bb | ave | econ | sr | 4w | 5w |
| 53 | 210 | 224 | 8 | 3/54 | 28.00 | 6.40 | 26.25 | 0 | 0 |

When Brendan Taylor made his first-class debut for Mashonaland A at the tender age of 15, he was considered a future Test star, but his promotion to the senior ranks just three years later still came as a surprise. Benefiting from the withdrawal of the "rebel" players, he made his international debut at the age of 18 as a middle-order batsman. When captain Tatenda Taibu retired from international cricket in 2005, Taylor took over the role of wicket-keeper and performed with much aplomb. With nine one-day half-centuries to his name, he has been one of the few shining lights in what has been an otherwise bleak period for Zimbabwe cricket.

followers were aware that Zimbabwe cricket would not, could not, be the same again.

Few inside their borders would be prepared to admit it, but life has been hard for Zimbabwe's cricketers post-Streak, Andy Flower and co. Failure followed failure and, amid growing calls for their demotion, they slipped to a demoralizing 3–2 series defeat to Bangladesh.

Desperate times call for desperate measures, and Heath Streak was recalled for the final one-day international against South Africa. He was Zimbabwe's best player by a country mile, but did not hang around long. By the end of the year he had accepted Warwickshire's captaincy offer and has not played for Zimbabwe since.

Streak's successor as captain, Tatenda Taibu, soon followed him out of the door. Tired of the press backlash following the string of poor results and facing a players' revolt, he retired from international cricket towards the end of 2005 at the age of just 22.

A drawn series with Kenya showed just how far Zimbabwe's cricket stock had fallen; it was compounded when they were hammered 5–0 in the West Indies. But when new captain Prosper Utseya led his team to a 3–2 series win over Bangladesh in August 2006, there was some cause for cheer.

It is difficult to know what will happen to Zimbabwe cricket when, or rather if, the dust settles from the political fallout. They will be desperate to perform well in the Caribbean: failure to do so could have catastrophic consequences for cricket in Zimbabwe.

# IRELAND

## GROUP D
### An Irish First

There was much rejoicing in 2005 when the cricketers of the Emerald Isle qualified for the 2007 World Cup in only their fourth attempt, and the Irish are a welcome addition to cricket's biggest showpiece.

Cricket has been played in the country since the 1880s and the Ireland cricket team, which like its rugby counterpart is represented by players from both north and south of the border, played first-class matches, most notably against the Scots, until 1999, and the odd tourists who found a gap in the calendar while touring England to hop over the Irish Sea.

Some would have wished they hadn't bothered, particularly the West Indies touring side of 1969. In a result that sent shockwaves around the world, the West Indies slumped to a nine-wicket defeat. Victims perhaps of the famous Irish hospitality the night before the match, the Caribbean kings capitulated to an embarrassing 25 all out.

The political problems that blighted Ireland for so many years had a huge impact on the development of Irish cricket. Indeed, it wasn't until 1993 that the ICC welcomed them into cricket's global family but, having attained associate member status, Ireland happily took their place in the following year's ICC Trophy in Kenya.

They won three of their group games to qualify for the second phase, but the step up in class showed and Ireland slumped to three heavy defeats. They embarked on the long journey home with plenty of food for thought.

Their performances in Malaysia three years later left even more room for contemplation. They eased through the initial group stages to qualify for the second phase. They then recorded a crucial victory over the Netherlands in a rain-affected match; a no result against Bangladesh and a comfortable win over Hong Kong followed. They had qualified for the semi-finals, and with three of the four remaining teams guaranteed a place in the 1999 World Cup, it was time to dream.

A semi-final loss against Kenya may not have been in the script, but it set up an intriguing showdown against Scotland for the final World

### WORLD CUP RECORD

World Cup debutants

Cup spot. And when they restricted the Scots to 187 for 8 hopes of victory would have remained high.

They were summarily smashed and Ireland slumped to 141 all out. Amid scenes of bitter disappointment, Irish World Cup dreams would have to be put on hold for at least another four years. Despite everything, they had proved they could compete with the best teams the ICC Trophy had to offer.

Hopes were high as the Irish travelled to

**Irish Aussie:** Consistently successful in Sydney grade cricket and a former bowler for New South Wales, Trent Johnston was welcomed into the Irish fold with open arms.

### FORM GUIDE – Last 3 ODIs

| | |
|---|---|
| Played: | 3 |
| Won: | 1 |
| Lost: | 1 |
| Tied: | 0 |
| No result: | 1 |
| Winning percentage: | 50% |
| Highest score: | 274 (v. Netherlands, Ayr, 8 August 2006) |
| Lowest score: | 240 (v. Scotland, Ayr, 5 August 2006) |
| Most runs conceded: | 301 (v. England, Belfast, 13 June 2006) |
| Runs scored per 6 balls: | 5.18 |
| Runs conceded per 6 balls: | 5.25 |

Canada for the 2001 ICC Trophy. It turned out to be another disappointing tournament: they scraped through to the Super League phase, but two victories, coupled with five defeats, saw their involvement in the competition come to a premature end.

If there was ever a chance to change their cricket fortunes, it would have been in front of their own fans when Ireland played host to the tournament four years later. With five places for the 2007 World Cup on offer, there was a sense of now or never for Ireland.

Ed Joyce was the star of the show for Ireland. The Middlesex batsman hit two centuries (103 v. Bermuda and 115 not out v. UAE) and a half-century (60 v. Denmark) as Ireland eased into the semi-finals. Their march to the last four had guaranteed their involvement in the Caribbean in 2007, meant that Ireland had gained one-day international status until 2009 and ensured $500,000 funding from the ICC. The party could begin and the icing on the cake would come if they could lift the ICC Trophy for the first time.

Peter Gillespie and Andrew White kept the dream alive, adding an unbroken seventh-wicket stand of 70 to haul their team to a nervy four-wicket win over Canada in the semi-finals.

Ireland would renew acquaintances with Scotland in the final.

However, just as had been the case in Malaysia eight years earlier, the Scots had the last laugh. Chasing a massive 325 for victory, Irish hopes fell with Ed Joyce's dismissal and the hosts slid to 277 for 9 and a 47-run defeat.

The disappointment of falling at the final hurdle was compounded by the knowledge that

Joyce, who finished the tournament with 399 runs at an average of 99.75, had pledged his future with England and would be unavailable to the Irish for the World Cup.

Ireland celebrated their one-day international status by welcoming England – with Joyce among their number – to Belfast in June 2006. Marcus Trescothick hit 113 as England compiled a formidable total of 301 for 9, but Ireland did not disgrace themselves: they may have lost, reaching 263 for 7, but they had done themselves proud. They then produced a morale-boosting 85-run win over their recent bogey team Scotland, with Eoin Morgan impressing with 99.

The Irish were the first side to name their World Cup squad, not out of over-excitement but through necessity; the majority of their team will have to arrange for work leave. They will no doubt find the step up in class difficult to cope with, but simply being there will be cause enough for Irish celebration.

# WELCOME TO THE WEST INDIES

Cricket in the West Indies has a power to which no other sport in the region can lay claim. The 38 million people who inhabit the islands that form a 2,000-mile (3,200km) breakwater – stretching from southern Florida to Venezuela on the South American coast – between the Caribbean Sea to the south and the Atlantic Ocean to the north stand united behind a single banner: the support of their beloved West Indian team.

West Indian cricket, like the region itself, took a while to gain its own identity: when it did, however, the cricket, like the islands themselves, rocked to the calypso beat. To read a who's who of the West Indies' best, is to read about some of the greatest players ever to have played the game.

# HISTORY OF WEST INDIES CRICKET

It would be no exaggeration to say that the impact the West Indies have made on world cricket is equal to the effect that Brazil have had on world football. For those growing up in the 1980s, the West Indies' style and flair showed the rest of the world how the game really should be played.

To read a list of the greatest players in the history of West Indian cricket is to name the game's greatest exponents, be it with bat or ball; players who achieved an iconic status and who changed the way the modern game is played. No greater compliment can be paid than to say that today's version of the game, with its crash-bang-wallop nature, can trace its origins to a collection of small islands in the Caribbean.

**Early star:** Along with George Headley, Learie Constantine was the first world-class cricketer to emerge from the Caribbean. He went on to a notable career in law and politics following his retirement from the game.

It wasn't always the case. In their early years of Test cricket, the West Indians struggled to assert themselves over their rivals. Memorable victories were often coupled with disappointing defeats, and it was individuals, rather than the team itself, that caught the public's gaze.

First came Learie Constantine, a ferocious batsman, a lightning-quick bowler, an electric fielder and a player capable of altering the course of a match.

Then there was George Headley. Such was his impact, he came to be known as the "Black Bradman", and England were the first on the receiving end of his batting genius when they played their first Test series in the Caribbean in

1928–29. Headley scored 176 in his debut Test. Three more centuries followed: he finished the series with 703 runs to his name (at an average of 87.87).

But Headley and Constantine could not carry the team on their own; when they failed, so did the West Indies. In some respects, it was as though the players – the team was still not exclusively all black – were mirroring the history of the islands from which they came: trying to break free from the shackles of their colonial past and trying to establish a style of their own.

The first players to do so came to be known collectively as the "Three Ws". As Test cricket resumed after the Second World War, Frank Worrell, Everton Weekes and Clyde Walcott would power the West Indian batting.

Walcott – who in 1960–61 would become the first black man to captain the West Indies for more than a single match – was an elegant, classy, right-hand bat, and an innings by the attacking Weekes was a joy to behold. Walcott was a giant of a man who could hit the ball with tremendous power, as England found to their cost at Lord's in 1950, when he smashed 168 not out in a West Indies victory. But Walcott wasn't the only player to shine in that particular match.

Given what was to come, the manner of that victory, and ultimately the series – for many it is the time West Indies cricket came of age – is surprising. There was barely a fast bowler in sight at Lord's in the second Test when Sonny Ramadhin (11 wickets in the match) and Alf Valentine (seven) spun the West Indies to a famous 322-run victory. It was the first time the home of cricket had echoed to the tune of the steel drum, but it would not be the last.

The visit of Pakistan to the Caribbean in 1957–58 provided the platform for a new West Indian hero to take centre stage. In the third Test at Kingston, 21-year-old Garfield Sobers smashed an unbeaten 365 to set a new mark in Test cricket, one that would stand for 36 years.

Sobers took his place in the West Indian team that toured Australia in 1960–61 in what is widely considered the best Test series of all time. At Brisbane in the first Test, Australia, set a victory target of 233, recovered from 92 for 6 and entered the final over needing six runs to win with three wickets in hand. They failed, and the Test was tied; it is one of only two instances of a tied Test match in the history of the game. Australia won the second match and the West Indies the third to set up a grand finale. The Aussies sneaked to a two-wicket victory in the final Test to take the series 2–1.

The following year, back in the Caribbean, the world saw the first glimpse of the formula that would make the West Indies the powerhouse of world cricket. Fast, hostile – the Indians called it "intimidatory" – bowling saw the home side sweep to a 5–0 series victory. The West Indians were becoming increasingly aware of the ingredients required for cricket dominance; they would have to wait some time before all the pieces fell into place.

In India, in 1973–74, Andy Roberts announced himself to the global cricket public by taking 32 wickets during the 3–2 series win. By 1976, Michael Holding had established himself in the line-up, destroying England with a devastating spell of 5 for 17 at Old Trafford.

With the bat, a young, gum-chewing Viv Richards, in his first innings against England, smashed a belligerent 232 and ended the West Indies' 3–0 series win with a mesmerizing 291 at The Oval. Desmond Haynes and Gordon Greenidge were establishing themselves as the most formidable opening batsmen in world cricket. Clive Lloyd was proving an astute and inspired leader and, by the time 6ft 8in Joel Garner joined the fray the following winter, the West Indies were the most formidable unit the game had ever seen.

They strolled to the first two World Cups (in 1975 and 1979). In 1983–84 they beat Australia 3–0 in a series remarkable for the fact that during the entirety of it, they did not lose a single second-innings wicket.

English cricket was left reeling when, in 1984, they suffered a 5–0 "blackwash". When Australia managed to draw the fourth Test at Melbourne in 1984–85, they stemmed the cascade of 11 successive defeats to the Caribbean kings. But England weren't so fortunate, crashing to a second successive blackwash when they travelled to the Caribbean in 1985–86.

Defeat against Pakistan the following year did not indicate a slide, merely a fall from dominance. Malcolm Marshall, Curtly Ambrose and Courtney Walsh slowly replaced Roberts, Holding and Garner: the West Indies still possessed some bowling "sting". But, by 1991, England had managed to draw (2–2) a series at home – a major achievement given that the score over the previous 15 Tests read 14–0 in the West Indies' favour – and, at last, the West Indies seemed beatable.

Viv Richards, still chewing no doubt, may have departed the scene, but a new prodigy was capturing the hearts of Caribbean cricket fans. In 1993–94, in the final Test against England in Antigua, Brian Lara smashed 375 to break Sobers's long-standing record. (Ten years later, when he hit an unbeaten 400, again against England and again in Antigua, he would set a new mark.)

Australia were stepping up to the mark. In 1994–95, the Aussies took the opening Test at Bridgetown to end the West Indies' dominant series of 20 wins and nine draws in their previous 29 Tests. When Australia took the deciding Test at Sabina Park by an innings and 53 runs, they inflicted the first series defeat on the West Indies for 15 years and the first on home soil for 22 years.

If defeat to Australia merely suggested that the West Indies had found a new sparring partner, then the 73-run defeat to lowly Kenya at the 1996 World Cup would have set alarm-balls ringing. The West Indies had entered a decline from which, to date, they still have not recovered.

As Australia went on to their own form of cricket global domination, the West Indies' slide

**Leading the way:** The first of the modern brand of West Indian fast bowlers was Andy Roberts. He took 32 wickets in the five-match Test series against India in 1973–74 and was soon joined in the side by Michael Holding.

down cricket's ladder became one of the most hotly debated topics in the game. There were still highs, such as the series wins over India (1–0) in 1996–97 and over England the following year (3–1), but there were also lows, some of them incomprehensible to all but the oldest of West Indian cricket fans, particularly when they slumped to a 5–0 whitewash against South Africa in 1998–99.

Their fall from grace was laid bare for all to see when they travelled to Australia in 2000–01. The home side took them apart, winning 5–0. To rub salt into an already considerable wound, they broke the West Indies' record of 11 consecutive Test wins during the course of the series.

West Indies cricket has yet to recover its former status, and there are those who argue it will never will. A nation's cricket hopes have risen from the ashes before though, and, in a country whose cricket legacy is so strong, there is every reason to believe that West Indian cricket fortunes will rise again. What better stage to do so than in the 2007 Cricket World Cup?

# THE PIRATES OF THE CARIBBEAN

Picture the stereotypical West Indian cricketer in your mind and you see the swashbuckling batsman, driving the ball majestically on the up, effortlessly whipping the ball through the legside from off stump, savagely cutting and hooking the ball towards the boundary ropes; or you see the tall fast bowler easing towards the stumps before unleashing a tracer missile-like bouncer rapidly honing in on the batsman's throat or the express yorker that rips out the middle stump and sends it somersaulting towards the slips. Dozens of Caribbean cricketers have exuded these qualities over the years; below are five who, above all, created the Calypso Cricket brand and showed the world how the game really should be played.

## GEORGE HEADLEY

| | |
|---|---|
| **Born:** | 30 May 1909, Colon, Panama |
| **Died:** | 30 November 1983, Kingston, Jamaica |
| **Role:** | Right-hand bat, leg-spin bowler |
| **Tests:** | 22 |
| **Debut:** | v. England, Bridgetown, 11–16 January 1930 |
| **Runs:** | 2,190 |
| **Highest score:** | 270 not out (v. England, Kingston, 14–18 March 1935) |
| **Average:** | 60.83 |
| **Hundreds:** | 10 |
| **Wickets:** | 0 |

Light on his feet and masterful off the back foot, George Headley was the first great black player to emerge from the West Indies. He made his Test debut against England in 1929–30, hitting 703 runs in the series at an average of 87.30, including 176 in the second innings of his debut Test. His scoring feats earned him the label the "Black Bradman". At Lord's in 1939, he became the first player to score a century in both innings of a Test and in Kingston in 1934–35, he scored a masterful unbeaten 270 against the touring English. His career effectively came to an end with the onset of the Second World War. His son Ron went on to play two Tests for the West Indies and, to complete a remarkable cricketing dynasty, his grandson Dean played 15 Tests for England.

## GARFIELD SOBERS

| | |
|---|---|
| **Born:** | 28 July 1936, Barbados |
| **Role:** | Left-hand bat, left-arm fast-medium/ slow left-arm |
| **Tests:** | 93 |
| **Debut:** | v. England, Kingston, 30 March–3 April 1954 |
| **Runs:** | 8,032 |
| **Highest score:** | 365 not out (v. Pakistan, Kingston, 26 February–4 March 1958 – six-day match) |
| **Average:** | 57.78 |
| **Hundreds:** | 26 |
| **Wickets:** | 235 |
| **Average:** | 34.03 |
| **Best bowling:** | 6 for 73 (v. Australia, Brisbane, 6–10 December 1968 ) |

Garfield Sobers was the finest all-round cricketer the game has ever seen. An elegant, powerful batsman, particularly through the offside, he was also an excellent bowler – who could bowl two types of spin (orthodox slow left arm and wrist spin) and a respectable fast-medium pace bowler – a supreme close-to-the-wicket fielder and an enterprising captain. Among his many fine achievements on a cricket field were his innings of 365 not out against Pakistan at Kingston in 1958; his six sixes off an over playing for Nottinghamshire against Glamorgan; and his innings of 254 for the Rest of the World v. Australia in 1971. He was knighted for his services to cricket in 1975.

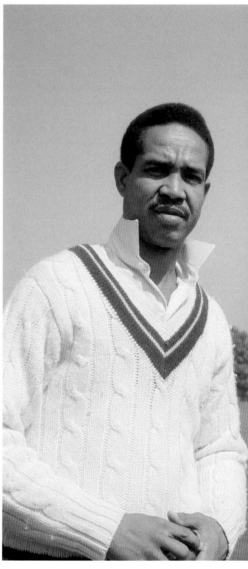

**One-man band:** Garfield Sobers was the best all-rounder ever.

## VIV RICHARDS

| | |
|---|---|
| **Born:** | 7 March 1952, Antigua |
| **Role:** | Right-hand bat, off-spin bowler |
| **Tests:** | 121 |
| **Debut:** | v. India, Bangalore, 22–27 November 1974 |
| **Runs:** | 8,540 |
| **Highest score:** | 291 (v. England, The Oval, 12–17 August 1976) |
| **Average:** | 50.23 |
| **Hundreds:** | 24 |
| **Wickets:** | 32 |
| **Average:** | 61.37 |
| **Best bowling:** | 2 for 17 (v. Pakistan, Port of Spain, 16–19 April 1988) |

Viv Richards brought a sense of swagger to the game like no player before or since. His gum-chewing slow amble to the crease belied the destruction he could wreak on opposition bowlers. He first made his mark in his debut series against India, hitting 192 in his second Test. Two years later, he scored 1,710 runs at an average of 90.00 with seven centuries in 11 Tests, still a record. He was also a highly successful captain; taking over from Clive Lloyd, he won 27 of his 50 matches at the helm. He was knighted for his services to cricket in 1999.

**Master blaster:** Viv Richards could destroy any attack.

## MALCOLM MARSHALL

| | |
|---|---|
| **Born:** | 18 April 1958, Barbados |
| **Died:** | 4 November 1999, Barbados |
| **Role:** | Right-hand bat, right-arm fast bowler |
| **Tests:** | 81 |
| **Debut:** | v. India, Bangalore, 15–20 December 1978 |
| **Runs:** | 1,810 |
| **Highest score:** | 92 (v. India, Kanpur, 21–25 October 1983) |
| **Average:** | 18.85 |
| **Hundreds:** | 0 |
| **Wickets:** | 376 |
| **Average:** | 20.94 |
| **Best bowling:** | 7 for 22 (v. England, Old Trafford, 30 June–5 July 1988) |

Malcolm Marshall was a master of both inswing and outswing and delivered the ball at an electrifying pace. Among the great fast bowlers to have emanated from the Caribbean, he was consistently the best. He came of age in England in 1980, taking 7 for 24 at Old Trafford, and in the space of two years was considered the best fast bowler on the planet. By the time he finished his Test career in 1991, he was the leading wicket-taker in West Indies history and still has the lowest average of any bowler to have taken over 200 Test wickets. Enormously popular, his death from cancer at the age of 41 shocked the cricket world.

**Simply the best:** Malcolm Marshall – scourge of all batsmen.

**Gentle giant:** His height made Curtly Ambrose a difficult proposition on any wicket.

## CURTLY AMBROSE

| | |
|---|---|
| **Born:** | 21 September 1963, Antigua |
| **Role:** | Left-hand bat, right-arm fast bowler |
| **Tests:** | 98 |
| **Debut:** | v. Pakistan, Georgetown, 2–6 April 1988 |
| **Runs:** | 1,439 |
| **Highest score:** | 53 (v. Australia, Port of Spain, 5–10 April 1991) |
| **Average:** | 12.40 |
| **Hundreds:** | 0 |
| **Wickets:** | 405 |
| **Average:** | 20.99 |
| **Best bowling:** | 8 for 45 (v. England, Barbados, 1990) |

Famous for his refusal to give interviews ("Curtly talk to no man"), the 6ft 7in Antiguan reserved his talking for the field of play. With an ability to extract steepling bounce from the slowest of pitches, he was capable of destroying opponents. The fifth bowler to pass the 400-wicket mark in Tests, he will be remembered for two stunning spells of bowling: his 6 for 24 at Trinidad in 1993–94 saw England crash to a paltry 46 all out; and his amazing burst of seven wickets for one run against Australia in Perth in 1992–93 secured the series for his side. Ambrose was a true giant of the game in every sense.

# TOURIST INFORMATION: THE HOST ISLANDS

**The Cricket World Cup will provide spectators with an opportunity to watch the world's greatest players plying their trade, but it will also provide people with a tourist experience that is second to none. Here is a quick rundown of all that the host islands have to offer their visitors.**

## ANTIGUA AND BARBUDA

| | |
|---|---|
| **Population:** | 72,000 (Antigua); 1,250 (Barbuda) |
| **Area:** | Antigua 108 sq miles (280 sq km); Barbuda 62 sq miles (160 sq km) |
| **Capital:** | St John's (Antigua); Codrington (Barbuda) |
| **Departure tax:** | Antigua US$50 |
| **Money:** | Eastern Caribbean dollar (EC$) |
| **Highlights:** | Half Moon Bay; Nelson's Dockyard; beaches; St John's; Codrington Lagoon, Barbuda |
| **Tourist info:** | www.antigua-barbuda.org |

There is a saying in Antigua that there is a beach for every day of the year and, above all, this is what makes the island one of the most popular tourist destinations in the Caribbean. Even though the nation gained its independence in 1981, Antigua still retains plenty of its British colonial traditions. The tall brick chimneys and decaying sugar mills that dot the island pay homage to a British heritage that dates back to the 1600s. As does the now-restored naval dockyard and the crumbling forts around the English Harbour and Shirley Heights. But where sugar once fuelled the island's economy, it is the tourists who now line the locals' pockets. Antigua is dotted with fantastic beaches, from Dickenson Bay in the northwest of the island to Half Moon Bay in the east and Rendezvous beach in the south; and for the more adventurous, the fabulous coral reefs offer wonderful scuba and snorkelling opportunities. If you'd prefer to get away from the tourists, Barbuda, Antigua's sister island, blessed with magnificent beaches and spectacular coral reefs, is just a 15-minute plane ride away: it's a journey well worth the effort.

## GRENADA

| | |
|---|---|
| **Population:** | 100,000 |
| **Area:** | 132 sq miles (344 sq km) |
| **Capital:** | St George's |
| **Departure tax:** | EC$50 (US$20) |
| **Money:** | Eastern Caribbean dollar (EC$) |
| **Highlights:** | Grand Anse beach; Bathway beach, Grand Etang National Park; Pearl's Airport; Mount Piton, Petite Martinique |
| **Tourist info:** | www.grenada.org |

The tiny nation of Grenada, which includes neighbouring Carriacou and Petite Martinique, is the southernmost of the Windward Islands. Aided by a gentle climate and extravagantly fertile volcanic soil, it is one of the largest producers of spices in the western hemisphere; its mass production of nutmeg, cinnamon, cloves, ginger, turmeric and mace gave it the nickname the "Island of Spice". That was before 2004, when the island suffered a direct hit from Hurricane Ivan. The crops were devastated and the island suffered major damage. Although repairs have been carried out and tourism is slowly getting back on its feet, the after-effects of Ivan still linger on. Paths in the Grand Etang National Park – a walker's paradise with a network of trails leading to picture-postcard waterfalls, crater lakes and mist-shrouded peaks – are still being cleared. But the beautiful white sand beaches, the most stunning of which is Grand Anse (a long horseshoe beach on the southwest tip of the island and the focus of the island's tourism) or the ruggedly beautiful Bathway beach, remain. As does the island's capital, St George's, one of the most charming and elegant towns in the Caribbean. If you feel like getting away from it

**Grand Etang National Park:** It may still be getting over the effects of 2004's Hurricane Ivan, but the rainforests and hidden waterfalls still astonish the visitor.

all, try out Carriacou, or Petite Martinique, an island dominated by the climbable Mount Piton at its centre, both just a short ferry ride away.

## GUYANA

| Population: | 751,000 |
|---|---|
| Area: | 83,000 sq miles (214,969 sq km) |
| Capital: | Georgetown |
| Departure tax: | n/a |
| Money: | Guyanese dollar (GY$) |
| Highlights: | Kaieteur Falls; Rupununi ranches; Amerindian village of Surama; Georgetown; Shanklands rainforest |
| Tourist info: | www.guyana.com |

Situated on the northern coast of South America, English-speaking, cricket-loving, rum-drinking Guyana is a largely undiscovered country that contains some of the world's most spectacular scenery. Ninety percent of the population live on the northern coastal plains, either in Georgetown or in the villages running eastwards towards Suriname. It is a country populated by six peoples: Africans, Amerindians, Chinese, East Indians, Europeans and Portuguese. "Guyana" is an Amerindian word meaning "Land of Many Waters", and water – or rather four rivers – dominates the landscape. The Demerara (the only river spanned by bridges), the Berbice, the Corentyne and the Essequibo (whose mouth is 21 miles (34km) wide). Inland from the coastal plains, most of the country is covered by rainforest – providing the tourist with wonderful trekking, bird- and animal-spotting opportunities. Towards the Venezuelan border to the east, the rainforest rises in a series of steep escarpments creating a land of dense forest and tumbling waterfalls. The most famous of these are the Kaieteur Falls, where the 400ft wide Potaro River plunges 822ft downward from the Pakaraima Plateau – it is the world's largest single-drop waterfall, five times the height of the Niagara Falls. In the southwest of the country is the Rupununi Savanna, an area of open grassland more easily reached from Brazil than from the capital Georgetown. For the less adventurous, Georgetown offers plenty of sights, including St George's Cathedral, one of the world's tallest free

standing wooden buildings, consecrated in 1892, or the famous Stabroek Market, once described as a "bizarre bazaar", which contains every conceivable item from household goods and gold jewellery to fresh meat and vegetables.

## JAMAICA

| Population: | 2.7 million |
|---|---|
| Area: | 4,400 sq miles (11,391 sq km) |
| Capital: | Kingston |
| Departure tax: | J$1000 (US$20) |
| Money: | Jamaican dollar (J$) |
| Highlights: | Bob Marley Mausoleum, Nine Mile; sunsets at Negril; Frenchman's cove; Blue Lagoon, Portland; Treasure Beach |
| Tourist info: | www.jamaicatravel.com |

Jamaica, among the most densely populated islands in the Caribbean, is one of the region's most popular tourist destinations. It may have a long history of social unrest and increasing levels of both crime and poverty, but Jamaica

**Dunn's River Waterfall:** One of the many marvels of Jamaica, this stunning waterfall attracts plenty of visitors, but is well worth the effort.

**Stir it up:** Take a trip up to Nine Mile to see the Bob Marley Museum and pay homage to the man who brought a global awareness to both reggae and Rastafarianism.

still swaggers to the rhythm of the reggae beat it invented. Despite increasing levels of tourism, its capital, Kingston, remains the country's pulsing centre. Home to more than a third of the island's 2.7 million people, and set against the backdrop of the stunning Blue Mountains – which offer wonderful hiking opportunities – it has a clubbing scene that is second to none. But the island is also ideal for those who want to go straight from the plane to the luxuries of an all-inclusive hotel for a bit of R&R. The tourist centres are located in the north of the island: Montego Bay (a busy commercial city close to Jamaica's most famous beaches), Ocho Rios (packed with shops, restaurants and bars) and Negril (on the west of the island, and the place to go to watch the setting sun as it sinks into the Caribbean Sea). There are equal rewards for those who want to leave the hotels behind them and explore: spectacular mountains and rivers, savannah plains strewn with cacti, and cascading waterfalls that tumble down 600ft of slippery rocks and ledges before spilling out on to the beach below.

## ST KITTS & NEVIS

| | |
|---|---|
| Population: | 35,000 (St Kitts); 11,000 (Nevis) |
| Area: | St Kitts: 68 sq miles (176 sq km); |
| | Nevis: 36 sq miles (93 sq km) |
| Capitals: | St Kitts: Basseterre; |
| | Nevis: Charlestown |
| Departure tax: | St Kitts: US$22 (US$5 for |
| | children under 12); Nevis: US$20.50 |
| Money: | Eastern Caribbean dollar (EC$) |
| Highlights: | Brimston Hill fortress, St Kitts; |
| | Plantation inns; Charlestown, Nevis; |
| | rainforests on the slopes of Mount |
| | Liamuiga, St Kitts; Nevis Peak |
| Tourist info: | www.stkitts-tourism.com |

St Kitts (short for Saint Christopher's) and Nevis comprise the smallest nation in the western hemisphere. The first English settlement in the Leeward Islands, and one of the richest sugar cane economies of the plantation age, St Kitts still retains a rich sense of British maritime history; Brimston Hill is one of the Caribbean's most impressive fortresses. The beaches here may not be as spectacular as in other parts of the Caribbean, but the marine life here is plentiful, and numerous wrecks off the island make this a great diving and snorkelling site. It is good for hiking, too, with trails heading through the inland rainforest, past waterfalls, towards the peak of 3,733ft (1,138m) Mount Liamuiga, a dormant volcanic peak. Also worth a look are the rambling plantation inns, many of which have been turned into charming hotels, the largest concentration of which can be found in the north of the island. St Kitts's sister island, Nevis, was spotted by Colombus on his second voyage to the region in 1493. He called it Nieves, Spanish for snow, because the island's cloud-covered islands reminded him of the Pyrenees.

## ST LUCIA

| | |
|---|---|
| Population: | 160,000 |
| Area: | 283 sq miles (616 sq km) |
| Capital: | Castries |
| Departure tax: | EC$54 |
| Money: | Eastern Caribbean dollar (EC$) |
| Highlights: | The Pitons; eastern nature trail; |
| | jungle biking in Anse Mamin; |
| | watching turtles by moonlight; bird |
| | watching in the St Lucian rainforest; |
| | La Soufrière sulphur springs; |
| | Balenbouche estate |
| Tourist info: | www.stlucia.org |

It seems strange, with its beautiful beaches, azure ocean – with numerous reefs and tropical fish – and rainforests that the volcanic island of St Lucia, the second largest of the Windward Islands, should have taken so long to attract any significant number of tourists. At the same time, its lower tourist profile is one of the island's greatest assets. The eminently missable capital, Castries, aside, it is an island fit for exploring. The western coast is lined with beautiful white and black sand beaches and quaint, untouched fishing villages. Further south you find the inviting town of Soufrière, dominated by the monolithic twin peaks of the Pitons, St Lucia's most famous sight. And then there is the rain-forested interior, rich in flora and fauna, home to numerous bird species and one of the rarest lizards in the world. For the better prepared, around a thousand visitors per year are allowed to experience the astonishing spectacle of leatherback turtles laying their eggs; it takes place every year from late March to late August. However, if shopping and nightlife are more your scene, you should head to the resort towns of the north. St Lucia's appeal lies in its contrast: for every luxurious hotel there is an intimate guesthouse; for every top-of-the-range restaurant there's a roadside shack. The island is one of the Caribbean's true treasures.

## ST VINCENT & THE GRENADINES

| | |
|---|---|
| Population: | 118,000 |
| Area: | 150 sq miles (389 sq km) |
| Capital: | Kingstown |
| Departure tax: | EC$40 |
| Money: | Eastern Caribbean dollar (EC$) |
| Highlights: | St Vincent's petroglyphs; La |
| | Soufrière; Bequia; inter-island |
| | ferries; Tobago Cays; Mustique |
| Tourist info: | www.svgtourism.com |

Offering a taste of the unspoilt Caribbean and situated 100 miles west of Barbados and nestled between St Lucia to the north and Grenada

**LEFT: Mustique:** Take it easy and soak up the splendour of one of the region's most exclusive islands.

**OPPOSITE: The Pitons of St Lucia:** Rising sharply from the Soufrière shoreline, the Pitons form one of the most distinctive landmarks in the Eastern Caribbean.

**Surf's up:** The Indian cricket team took time out from their 2006 tour to the Caribbean to check out the surf on Barbados's east coast; it provides some of the best surfing in the world.

to the south, St Vincent and the Grenadines is a string of more than 30 islands, varying in character, terrain and appeal, that have long been cherished by divers and yachtsmen for their natural beauty. St Vincent, the largest and most fertile island in the country, is the main centre of the nation's activity, even though it has been relatively untouched by tourism. The island has two distinct coastlines: rugged and windswept in the east, gentle and idyllic on the west. A visit into St Vincent's lush interior is a must, as is a climb through the rainforests to the peak of La Soufrière, the island's active volcano. The less populated islands that form part of the chain are all easily accessible by ferry. Don't miss the chance to spend some time on the tiny island of Bequia, a paradise for sailing fanatics and the centre of the nation's boat-building communities. Or take a day trip to Mustique, the long-time home of Princess Margaret and still a hideaway for the rich and famous. However, expect your wallet to feel considerably lighter should you choose to spend the night in one of the island's luxurious hotels.

## BARBADOS

| | |
|---|---|
| **Population:** | 280,000 |
| **Area:** | 166 sq miles (430 sq kms) |
| **Capital:** | Bridgetown |
| **Departure tax:** | B$25 (for stays over 24 hours) |
| **Money:** | Barbados dollar (B$) |
| **Highlights:** | Andromeda botanical gardens; plantation houses; rum shops; flying fish sandwiches; surfing at Bathsheba |
| **Tourist info:** | www.barbados.org |

A staunchly loyal member of the Commonwealth and a British colony for over three centuries, Barbados has been described as a great coral reef floating in the mid-Atlantic. It is a place of contrast, from the giant waves that crash into its east coast, to the rolling hills in the centre of the island and the densely populated flatlands of the south and west. It is an island with a distinctly British feel, from the place names, the Anglican parish churches to the impressive range of colonial sites that scatter the island, with the old plantation houses and the military forts at Gun Hill and Grenade Hill still major tourist attractions. But Barbados is very much West Indian country: its people are fiercely proud, there are rum shops aplenty, calypso is the music of choice and flying fish are still the preferred dish of the day. Its capital Bridgetown possesses

an array of bars and restaurants. Speightstown, once a thriving and wealthy port, is now a great place to drink a rum cocktail on terraces overlooking the sea. There are beaches aplenty; the most popular are Accra beach and Mullins Bay, but head to the southeast of the island to find your own quieter patch of paradise. The rugged, relatively unexplored east coast, although bad for swimming, is excellent for surfing.

## TRINIDAD & TOBAGO

| | |
|---|---|
| **Population:** | 1.3 million |
| **Area:** | Trinidad: 5,128 sq miles (13,281 sq km); Tobago: 300 sq miles (777 sq km) |
| **Capital:** | Port of Spain |
| **Departure tax:** | TT$100 |
| **Money:** | Trinidad and Tobago dollar (TT$) |
| **Highlights:** | Northern range, Trinidad; Caroni swamp; bird sanctuary; leatherback turtles; diving and snorkelling in Tobago; Trinidad street food |
| **Tourist info:** | www.visittnt.com |

The southernmost of the West Indian nations, lying just 6¾ miles (11km) off the coast of South America, Trinidad and Tobago is the most industrial of the Caribbean nations, the most influential in the eastern Caribbean and the most diverse and absorbing culture in the region. Because of its reserves of natural gas and oil, it is not as dependent on the tourist trade as many of its Caribbean neighbours, but it remains a delightful place to visit. Its capital, Port of Spain, with its grand architecture, is the transport hub of Trinidad. From there you should explore the northern range (excellent for hiking) and the undisturbed tropical rainforests. You can take a boat ride through mangrove swamps, watch leatherback turtles lay their eggs on remote beaches, or catch a glimpse of one of the 430 bird species that live on the island. Its uncontrived, under-explored nature makes Trinidad one of the most exciting West Indian islands. If it's beaches you're after, head to Tobago, 20 miles (30 km) northeast of its sister island. It is blessed with many beautiful white sand beaches and, containing the largest brain coral in the world, has been dubbed the "Disneyland of Diving".

# A TASTE OF THE CARIBBEAN

As varied as the cultures that have called these islands home, food in the Caribbean is a hybrid of concoctions that can delight the western palate. What's more, there's an abundance of delicious options to quench the thirst: fresh, tropical fruit which, for the more daring, can be combined with local rum – or other spirits – to produce some memorable cocktails; or a selection of quality, locally produced lager that is instantly refreshing and which provides a worthy toast to any of the spectacular sunsets.

## FOOD

West Indian food draws from a blend of African, Indian, Arab, Chinese, Spanish, French, Dutch and British influences, although most of the islands have their own leanings and don't be surprised to find the same fare on offer in top-of-the-range restaurants and local street stalls.

There are some very distinct styles of cooking throughout the Caribbean region:

**Criollo** – popular in the Spanish-speaking islands, such as Puerto Rico, Cuba and the Dominican Republic, and which makes liberal use of cilantro and mixed seasonings like adobo.

**Indonesian** – predominates in the Dutch-speaking areas of the Netherlands Antilles, and in which soy sauce, satay and nasi goreng are prevalent.

**French** – although most colonies have a tendency to cook in the creole style, in the French-speaking areas (Martinique and Guadeloupe) you will often find delicious sauces made from chives, bouquet garni and tomato and applied liberally to fish and chicken.

**Jerk cooking** – a style common throughout the Caribbean which takes its origins from the African slaves who came to Jamaica in the 1600s. The meat is coated in a mixture of spices, including ginger, thyme, pimento, hot peppers and green onion, and is then cooked slowly in a pit or over a barbecue grill. As legend has it, it was invented by runaway slaves who cooked their meat in earth pits covered with branches to prevent detection from their pursuers.

**Indian** – the influence is unmistakable in the curries of Trinidad. "Rotis", chapatti envelopes filled with curried meat, seafood or vegetables, are now becoming common fare throughout the Caribbean. Indeed, dishes of curried goat and chicken have spread as far as the British islands.

**Spanish** – the Puerto Rican specialities of *lechón asoa* (roast suckling pig), and *lorico* (a variation of paella) in the Dominican Republic, both bear the hallmarks of a Spanish colonial past. The flavours tend to be more savoury than spicy. For example, in Cuba, the use of lime and garlic is more prevalent than pimento (a variety of chilli pepper made into a sauce), which is used liberally elsewhere in the Caribbean. Other common flavours in Spanish-speaking areas are cinnamon and nutmeg.

These stand alongside the staple foods, such as rice 'n' peas (actually red kidney beans), fried plantains (a variety of banana that is inedible raw), callaloo (a spinach-type vegetable), breadfruit, and root vegetables (yam, eddoe and cassava).

Meat, other than the ubiquitous goat, is often expensive. Seafood, on the other hand, is excellent, cheap and everywhere. Millions of holidaymakers will have wonderful memories of the day they went to a restaurant and ordered freshly caught fish, straight from the nets and shimmering with seawater, before it is placed on a sizzling barbecue and drizzled with fresh lime. Lobster, prawns, shrimps, red snapper, blue

**Eating al fresco:** Roadside jerk chicken vendors sell their wares on many street corners and the food there can be as good as that found in many of the top-of-the-range hotels.

# CARIBBEAN COCKTAILS

Why not get in the mood with a West Indian-style evening? Turn up the central heating, don a pair of shorts or a bikini and sample a taste of the Caribbean with the following cocktails.

### CARIBBEAN BEACH PARTY:
2 oz (60 ml) Light Rum
2 oz (60 ml) Triple sec
2 oz (60 ml) cherry liqueur
2 oz (60 ml) Crème de Banane
2 oz (60 ml) Malibu
8 oz (250 ml) pineapple juice
8 oz (250 ml) cranberry juice
ice

**Mixing instructions:**
This will get any party going. Half-fill a punch bowl with ice, pour in all the ingredients and stir thoroughly.

### CARIBBEAN BREEZE:
1/2 oz (15 ml) Light Rum
1/2 oz (15 ml) cherry liqueur
1/2 oz (15 ml) Crème de Banane
1/2 oz (15 ml) Malibu
5 oz (150 ml) lemonade
5 oz (150 ml) pineapple juice
ice

**Mixing instructions:**
Put the ice in a Collins glass and pour the remaining ingredients into a shaker, shake, then pour over the ice.

### CARIBBEAN CHAMPAGNE:
1 oz (30 ml) White Rum
1 oz (30 ml) Crème de Banane
fill with chilled Champagne
ice

**Mixing instructions:**
Pour the rum and the crème de banane into a champagne flute. Fill up with champagne, stir, and serve.

### CARIBBEAN FREEZE (non alcoholic):
2 oz (60 ml) cherry mix
2 oz (60 ml) banana mix
1 oz (30 ml) pina colada mix
1 oz (30 ml) cream
2 scoops ice cream
ice

**Mixing instructions:**
Place all the ingredients in a shaker and blend until smooth. Pour into a Collins glass. To make this an alcoholic drink, use Cherry Schnapps, Crème de Banane and Malibu instead of the mixes. You can also use fruit sorbet or fruit ice creams to make different flavours.

### CARIBBEAN MARGARITA:
3 oz (90 ml) Rum
1 oz (30 ml) Triple sec
1 oz (30 ml) lime juice
salt

**Mixing instructions:**
Rub the rim of cocktail glass with lime juice and dip rim in salt. Shake all ingredients with ice, strain into the salt-rimmed glass and serve.

Alternatives: For a regular Margarita use Tequila instead of rum. For fruit margaritas, and depending on how strong you like your margaritas, add 2 oz (60 ml) Schnapps or cherry cordial/mix for a cherry, crème de pêche or peach mix/cordial (peach), crème de mur or blackberry mix/cordial (blackberry), raspberry schnapps/Chambord or raspberry mix/cordial (raspberry), crème de fraise or strawberry cordial (strawberry), mango cordial or wildberry schnapps.

### CARIBBEAN PUNCH:
Crushed brown sugar
Peel of 1 Orange
2 pints (1 litre) Still mineral water
7 oz (200 ml) Light rum
7 oz (210 ml) Dark rum
2 pints (1 litre) Pineapple juice
2 pints (1 litre) Mango juice
2 pints (1 litre) Orange juice
Juice of 3 Limes squeezed
Chunks of Pineapple
Chunks of Mango
Chunks of Orange
Grated Nutmeg

**Mixing instructions:**
The beauty of any punch is that almost any ingredients can be used. You will find that on each of the islands, the locals will make their own variation of a punch. This one is rather special. Make a sugar syrup by boiling the brown sugar, water and orange peel for 30 minutes, then allow it to cool. Stir it together with the other ingredients in a large bowl. Garnish with chunks of pineapple, mango and orange, and sprinkle with freshly grated nutmeg before serving.

Alternative: For a non-alcoholic punch, leave out the rums.

**Each to their own:** Ranging in taste and strength, most of the islands will brew their own brand of lager. Some brands, however, are more widely available than others.

marlin, kingfish and flying fish can all be found cooked in this way.

Those with an adventurous leaning should try out the local weekend fish fries, where freshly caught fish are cooked by the roadside (grilled on barbecues or fried) and served with grilled patties of unleavened bread.

Soups and stews are abundant throughout the region. They may all be variations on a theme, but all are incomplete without a bottle of Caribbean pepper sauce; developed by the Carib and Arawak Indians, it consists of hot peppers, cassava juice, brown sugar, cloves and cinnamon to produce a thick, tangy sauce that is liberally sprinkled over barbecued fish or chicken.

The lush tropical vegetation provides a stunning array of fruit. Coconuts, pineapples, mangos, limes, melons, passion fruits, pomegranates and figs are old friends, but some exotic fruits, many of which are too fragile to be exported from the Caribbean, may be unfamiliar to the first-time tourist. These include breadfruit, ugli, naseberry, tamarind, sapodilla, soursop, plantains, cherimoya, monstera, loquat, carambola, guava, and mamey sapote.

It may be down to the abundance of sugar cane in the region, but desserts play an important part in the Caribbean meal. They come in all shapes and sizes, from dumplings, cakes and rice puddings to flans, mousses and soufflés. Not forgetting the ice creams and sorbets, or the dried or fresh fruit that has been liberally sprinkled with local rum.

## DRINK

It may come as little surprise given that the Caribbean is the rum capital of the world, but the spirit is the tipple of choice for most of the islanders and the drink plays an integral part in Caribbean life; even the smallest of villages will have a rum shop and rarely a day will pass where you don't see old men nursing their glasses of over-proof "whites" and putting the world to rights.

Rum has been produced in the Caribbean since the 17th century, when sugar planters first distilled a spirit from molasses. They added yeast to the sugar cane to start the fermentation process (sucrose turns to alcohol). The "dead wash" is then boiled and the evaporating alcohol is collected. After a little blending and the addition of some water, the white rums are ready to bottle; the smoother brown rums are aged in oak barrels, which give them their colour.

The best-quality rums traditionally come from Barbados, Jamaica, Martinique and Guadeloupe, but it is ubiquitous through the islands. Most locals prefer to drink their rum neat and drinking a seven-year-old añejo with ice and watching the sun sink lazily into the Caribbean Sea can be as good as life gets.

Other distinctly Caribbean drinks include:
- The "mauby", made from the bark of a tree and which tastes a bit like an exotic sarsaparilla.
- "Irish moss", or "sea moss" which is made by extracting gelatin from seaweed, adding sweetener, and combining the mixture with milk or ginger.
- Coconut water, which comes from the meat of the nut, is not to be confused with coconut milk or coconut cream. It's found on virtually every corner of every island market. Coconuts are abundant, inexpensive, and safe and fun to drink.
- Ginger beer, a soft drink variation from Trinidad.
- "Ting", a grapefruit-based sweet drink that can be found on many of the islands.

But the vast majority of tourists are more tempted by the long list of rum-based cocktails. These include piña coladas (with pineapple and coconut), Cuba libre (with cola), fruit daiquiris and planters' punch (the original only has lime and cane juice, but fruit juices are often added today).

If spirits aren't your thing, the moderately light, local beers provide a refreshing alternative. Somewhere between their European and American counterparts in strength, the most popular are Jamaica's Red Stripe, St Lucia's aptly named Piton Lager and the regional favourite, Carib beer, brewed in Trinidad and Tobago. Alternatives include Wadadli (a pale lager brewed in Antigua), Banks Beer (from Barbados), Kalik (the Bahamian brew) and Kubuli, which is made from Dominican springwater.

Guinness is also popular on the British islands, but warming as it is on a cold, crisp winter's night in northern Europe, its heavy nature somehow feels less palatable under the tropical sun.

The same can't be said for fruit juice, a great alcohol-free alternative. The Caribbean region also produces some of the world's finest coffee. Jamaica's Blue Mountain coffee is already well established in the global marketplace, but Haitian Blue is fast gaining a reputation among coffee connoisseurs.

# WORLD CUP HISTORY

The Cricket World Cup may not be to the purists' taste, but even the most sceptical of the sport's fans would find it hard to argue against the fact that the tournament has become a huge international hit. The only real surprise was that it took so long for this hugely popular form of cricket at club level to move on to the international stage, but ever since the inaugural competition in England in 1975, the Cricket World Cup has provided a spectacular platform upon which the best teams and the greatest players have thrilled a global audience of millions.

**Global game!** The inaugural Cricket World Cup in 1975 brought not only the short format of the game to a wider audience, it confirmed the diversity and passion of global cricket fans.

# WE ARE THE CHAMPIONS

The inaugural World Cup match was played at Lord's on a gorgeous early June day. Anyone who hasn't watched a match since probably will not recognize the entertainment at Sabina Park on 13 March 2007. For them, this is a brief recap of the eight World Cup competitions.

## 1975: ENGLAND
### Caribbean carnival

For a while, it seemed that cricket's greatest event would never get off the ground. That it did was thanks to England who, surprisingly, were the only country willing to offer the resources to stage what would be cricket's greatest event. The cricketing world was glad they did: the tournament introduced television audiences to a brand-new cricketing crowd and, arguably, the game would never be the same again. Accompanied by horn-blowing, can-rattling, reggae-loving fans, the West Indies, helped by their cohort of tear-away fast bowlers and swashbuckling batsmen, cut a swathe through the tournament on their way to claiming the game's ultimate prize. Three wins in their group games, against Sri Lanka (by nine wickets), Pakistan (by one wicket) and Australia (by seven wickets) saw them ease into the semi-finals. England's march to the title ended in disappointing fashion at the semi-final stage, where they capitulated to a sorry 93 all out against Australia, with Gary Gilmour ripping through

**Perfect timing:** Clive Lloyd often had to curb his attacking instincts to haul his side out of trouble. His 102 in the 1975 World Cup final paved the way for a West Indian victory.

### CLIVE LLOYD

A tall, hard-hitting left-hander, Clive Lloyd's astute leadership led the West Indies to the very pinnacle of world cricket for almost two decades. He scored only one century in his 87 one-day internationals, but his timing was perfect: his 102 in the 1975 World Cup final helped his side to victory.

### 1975 World Cup Final at Lord's, 21 June

West Indies 291 for 8 (60 overs) (CH Lloyd 102, RB Kanhai 55, GJ Gilmour 5 for 48)
Australia 274 (58.4 overs) (IM Chappell 62, KD Boyce 4 for 50)
**West Indies won by 17 runs**
**Man of the Match:** CH Lloyd

the England batting line-up with 6 for 14. The Australian left-arm seamer took another five wickets in the final, but the West Indies' total of 291 for 8, with Clive Lloyd (102) – ably assisted by Rohan Kanhai (55) – leading from the front in cavalier fashion, proved too much for the Aussies, who fell 17 runs short. A young Viv Richards also played his part, with three run outs.

## 1979: ENGLAND
### Two in a row

Although the inaugural World Cup had grabbed the attention of the public, the second offering, staged once again in England, was hardly greeted by a fanfare from the television companies. Played under the heavy cloud of World Series cricket

### JOEL GARNER

There can have been few more intimidating visions for batsmen between 1977 and 1987 than the sight of the 6ft 8in Joel Garner thundering towards the crease. Capable of extracting lethal bounce and possessing one of the most devastating yorkers the game has ever seen, "Big Bird" took 146 wickets in 98 one-day internationals and also excelled in the Test arena, with 259 wickets to his name.

### 1979 World Cup Final at Lord's, 23 June

West Indies 286 for 9 (60 overs) (IVA Richards 138*, CL King 86)
England 194 (51 overs) (JM Brearley 54, G Boycott 57, J Garner 5 for 38)
**West Indies won by 92 runs**
**Man of the Match:** IVA Richards

and the Packer era, it turned out to be an almost endless summer of cricket, with the ICC Trophy, the non-Test playing countries' world championship, providing an almost seamless link to the main event. The top two sides from the ICC – Sri Lanka and Canada – then formed part of the World Cup proper draw, with Sri Lanka causing a stir when they beat India in a group game. England made it to the final where they came up against Viv Richards (138 not out) and Collis King (86), who shared a swashbuckling stand of 139 in 21 overs to lead the defending champions to 286 for 9. It was always going to be tough going for England and an obdurate, but slow, opening partnership of 129 between Mike Brearley and Geoff Boycott was rendered meaningless by the searing pace of Joel Garner, who produced a burst of five wickets in 11 balls to send the hosts crashing to 194 all out. The West Indies had eased to their second World Cup in a row and became the team to beat in both forms of the game.

## 1983: ENGLAND
### An Indian summer

Staged in England for the third successive time and with eight teams – Sri Lanka and Zimbabwe joined the six Test-playing countries – the tournament's popularity was evident. Crowd attendances were up 100,000 on the previous tournament and profits reached the £1 million mark for the first time.

When Zimbabwe beat Australia in their opening group game at Trent Bridge, it was becoming clear that this was going to be a tournament of surprises. And Zimbabwe's one shock victory almost became two before Kapil Dev rescued India (struggling on 17 for 5) with a majestic, unbeaten 175 to guide them to victory. With confidence restored, India went on to beat Australia in their final group game and qualified for the semi-finals at the Aussies' expense. Then came Old Trafford and England; India, on an agonizingly slow pitch, prevailed by six wickets, with Yashpal Sharma top scoring for the Indians with 61.

To face them in the final, and to the surprise of no one, were the West Indies, seeking their third World Cup in a row. And with India skittled for 183, everything was going according to the pre-tournament script. However, Mohinder Armanath and Madan Lal failed to learn their lines; each took three wickets, the West Indies capitulated to 140 all out, and India had broken the World Cup's Caribbean monopoly.

### KAPIL DEV

Easily the best fast bowler India has ever produced, Kapil Dev was also its finest all-rounder. He reserved his best performances for India's 1983 World Cup success – his unbeaten 175 saved them against Kenya – but he went on to captain his country and finished his career with a record haul of Test wickets (434).

### 1983 World Cup Final at Lord's, 25 June

**India 183** (54.4 overs)
**West Indies 140** (52 overs)
**India won by 43 runs**
**Man of the Match:** M Armanath

## 1987: INDIA/PAKISTAN
### Australia take the crown

England may be the home of cricket but, in terms of sheer popularity, the game's spiritual home may well be in the subcontinent. Where better then to stage the fourth Cricket World Cup than in India and Pakistan? The choice may have produced its critics, but even they were blown into submission when 50,000 cricket-mad locals crammed into Eden Gardens to watch a routine group match between Zimbabwe and New Zealand. And carried along by the crest of euphoria sweeping the host countries, both India and Pakistan made it to the semi-finals. In Bombay, England, led by a masterly knock of 115 by Graham Gooch – who swept the Indian spinners, and the crowd, to despair – reached an imposing total of 254 for 6 off their 50 overs. It was too much for the home side and they fell 36 runs short. In Lahore, where Pakistan faced Australia, the joint hosts seemed well on their way to victory until five wickets from Craig McDermott reduced them to an 18-run defeat. England, on 135 for 2, chasing 254 for victory, seemed well on their way to their target until skipper Mike Gatting was dismissed by his Aussie counterpart Allan Border.

**Moment of madness:** A disgruntled Mike Gatting leaves the fray after falling to Allan Border. His inexplicable reverse-sweep was undoubtedly the major turning point of the the final.

### ALLAN BORDER

An obdurate batsman and a canny, if reluctant, captain, Allan Border guided his team to World Cup success in 1987, to the recapture of the Ashes two years later and to the start of a period of unrivalled dominance thereafter. He retired having led his country in a record 93 Tests.

### 1987 World Cup Final at Calcutta, 8 November

**Australia 253 for 5** (50 overs) (DC Boon 75)
**England 246 for 8** (50 overs) (CWJ Athey 58)
**Australia won by 7 runs**
**Man of the Match:** DC Boon

England never recovered, finishing eight runs short, and Australia had become the champions of the world.

## 1992: NEW ZEALAND
### Imran inspires Pakistan to the title

With the tournament's popularity never higher, it was Australia, the defending champions, and New Zealand, who hosted the fifth World Cup. Retaining the 50-over format and with coloured clothing and floodlights used for the first time, each team – including late entrants post-apartheid South Africa – played the others in the group

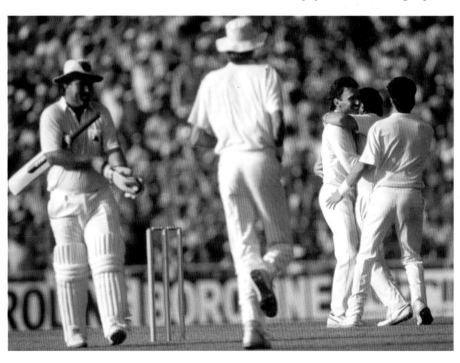

stage with the four best teams advancing to the semi-finals. After a series of shock results, weather interruptions and sensational cricket, New Zealand, Pakistan, England and South Africa advanced; guaranteeing there would be a new name on the trophy. Pakistan eased past the stunned hosts in Auckland in the first semi-final;

**Not this time:** Derek Pringle survives an lbw shout, but Man of the Match Wasim Akram had already taken two wickets in two balls to rip the heart out of England's middle order.

the other proved a controversial affair. The South Africans, chasing 253, needed 22 off 13 balls when rain interrupted play for 12 minutes. A new target would have to be calculated. When the players took to the field, the new requirement was flashed on the scorecard: 21 off one ball. England, with a huge slice of luck, had made it to the final. But it was Pakistan who shone: Javed Miandad and Imran Khan eased them to a defendable total (249 for 6) and their bowlers, led by an inspired Wasim Akram (3 for 49), eased Pakistan to a 22-run victory and their finest hour.

## 1996: INDIA/PAKISTAN/SRI LANKA
### Sri Lanka shock the world

There was much debate about the choice of India, Pakistan and Sri Lanka as joint hosts. As the tournament approached, so the threat of terrorist bombs in Colombo grew and both Australia and the West Indies forfeited their games against Sri Lanka. With the number of competing teams now up to 12 – Kenya, the United Arab Emirates and Holland joined the fray – the top eight duly qualified for the quarter-finals. Although not without alarm: the West Indies fell to 93 all out against the amateur bowlers of Kenya. Sri Lanka, India, Australia and the West Indies made it into the last four. The first of the semi-finals, between India and Sri Lanka, was a riot … literally. An

element of the 100,000-strong home support, angered by their side's inability to chase down Sri Lanka's 251 for 8, started to throw things on to the pitch and, worse, light fires in the stands. India were 120 for 8 when the players were led off the field and the match was awarded to Sri Lanka, who would face Australia in the final. The Aussies' total of 241 for 7 in Lahore was an above-average score, but no more. And so it proved, as Aravinda de Silva, with a spectacular century (107 not out), led his side to a majestic victory with over three overs to spare.

## 1999: ENGLAND
### Australia come good

With the number of participating countries still at 12, the teams were split into two groups with the top three progressing to a new Super Six stage. The hosts did not make it that far. Despite an encouraging opening victory against Sri Lanka, crushing defeats to South Africa and India left them trailing Zimbabwe on run-rate. The African nation were joined in the Super Six by India, South Africa, New Zealand, Pakistan and Australia, who had barely scraped through and who needed to find their form fast. They did, winning every game, and qualified for the semi-finals, along with Pakistan, New Zealand and South Africa. Pakistan eased to victory in the first semi-final against New Zealand, but it was the second semi-final that has entered cricket lore. South Africa, chasing

**One last hurrah:** Shane Warne may not have know it at the time, but the 1999 final at Lord's would be the great leg-spinner's final appearance in the Cricket World Cup.

214 for victory, were taken to the brink of victory by Lance Klusener. With three balls remaining, and the scores tied, Klusener called for a single, Allan Donald stood his ground and was run out. Australia won by virtue of losing fewer wickets. However, the Aussies were as skilful in the final as they had been fortunate in the last four. With Shane Warne at his best, Pakistan subsided to 132 all out and Australia cantered to the total with nearly 30 overs to spare.

## 2003: SOUTH AFRICA/ZIMBABWE/ KENYA
### Australia on top of the world

It was good news that the tournament made the headlines long before it started. But it was bad news that the stories were barely cricket-related ones. With political tension rife – England and New Zealand forfeited their games against Zimbabwe and Kenya respectively and Shane Warne, Australia's leading light, tested positive for a diuretic – it was a relief when the cricket finally started. Not for the hosts South Africa, though, who were among a number of high-profile teams to fall at the group stage, along with England and Pakistan. Against all pre-tournament expectations, Kenya beat Zimbabwe in their Super Six match to book a place in the semi-final against India, whose total of 270 proved too much for them and they slipped to 179 all out. India were joined in the final by

Australia, who completed a comprehensive 43-run win over Sri Lanka. The final was all about Australia and Ricky Ponting, who hit a magnificent unbeaten 140 to see his side to 359 for 2. When Glenn McGrath dismissed Sachin Tendulkar in the first over, India's fate was virtually sealed; they eventually subsided to 234 all out in the 40th over and Australia were world champions for the third time.

**The team to beat:** Australia were at the height of their powers in South Africa in 2003. They marched through the tournament unbeaten and rarely troubled on the way to retaining their crown.

# WORLD CUP RECORDS

They say that records are there to be broken, and many of the Cricket World Cup's record-breakers will be making their way to the Caribbean looking for another shot at glory. India's Sachin Tendulkar will be hoping to add to his record-breaking tally of runs; Glenn McGrath will be seeking to repeat his 2003 match-winning bowling performance against Namibia; Ricky Ponting will be looking to add to his collection of catches. But who is the oldest player to have played in the Cricket World Cup? What is the best partnership? Who holds the record for the highest individual score? Who has played in the most matches? The answers to those questions and many more can be found in the next few pages...

**Wasim Akram:** No one has taken more Cricket World Cup wickets, although a successful 2007 tournament for Glenn McGrath will see him challenge the record...

# THE TOP PERFORMANCES

The World Cup may not be to the cricket purists' taste, but over the years the tournament has provided a spectacular stage for the game's greatest players and has thrilled a global audience of millions.

## OVERALL TEAM WORLD CUP RECORDS

| Team | Mts | Won | Lost | Tied | NR | Win % |
|---|---|---|---|---|---|---|
| Australia | 58 | 40 | 17 | 1 | 0 | 68.96 |
| West Indies | 48 | 31 | 16 | 0 | 1 | 65.95 |
| South Africa | 30 | 19 | 9 | 2 | 0 | 63.33 |
| England | 50 | 31 | 18 | 0 | 1 | 63.26 |
| India | 55 | 31 | 23 | 0 | 1 | 57.40 |
| Pakistan | 53 | 29 | 22 | 0 | 2 | 56.86 |
| New Zealand | 52 | 28 | 23 | 0 | 1 | 54.90 |
| Sri Lanka | 46 | 17 | 27 | 1 | 1 | 37.77 |
| Kenya | 20 | 5 | 14 | 0 | 1 | 26.31 |
| Zimbabwe | 42 | 8 | 31 | 0 | 3 | 20.51 |
| Bangladesh | 11 | 2 | 8 | 0 | 1 | 20.00 |
| United Arab Emirates | 5 | 1 | 4 | 0 | 0 | 20.00 |
| Canada | 9 | 1 | 8 | 0 | 0 | 11.11 |
| Netherlands | 11 | 1 | 10 | 0 | 0 | 9.09 |
| East Africa | 3 | 0 | 3 | 0 | 0 | 0.00 |
| Namibia | 6 | 0 | 6 | 0 | 0 | 0.00 |
| Scotland | 5 | 0 | 5 | 0 | 0 | 0.00 |

## HIGHEST INDIVIDUAL SCORES

| | | |
|---|---|---|
| 188* | G Kirsten | South Africa v. United Arab Emirates, Rawalpindi, 1996 |
| 183 | SC Ganguly | India v. Sri Lanka, Taunton, 1999 |
| 181 | IVA Richards | West Indies v. Sri Lanka, Karachi, 1987 |
| 175* | Kapil Dev | India v. Zimbabwe, Tunbridge Wells, 1983 |
| 172* | CB Wishart | Zimbabwe v. Namibia, Harare, 2003 |
| 171* | GM Turner | New Zealand v. East Africa, Birmingham, 1975 |
| 161 | AC Hudson | South Africa v. Netherlands, Rawalpindi, 1996 |
| 152 | SR Tendulkar | India v. Namibia, Pietermaritzburg, 2003 |
| 145 | R Dravid | India v. Sri Lanka, Taunton, 1999 |
| 145 | PA de Silva | Sri Lanka v. Kenya, Kandy, 1996 |

## BATTING: MOST RUNS

| Name | Mat | I | NO | Runs | HS | Ave | SR | 100 | 50 |
|---|---|---|---|---|---|---|---|---|---|
| SR Tendulkar | 33 | 32 | 3 | 1732 | 152 | 59.72 | 87.56 | 4 | 12 |
| Javed Miandad | 33 | 30 | 5 | 1083 | 103 | 43.32 | 67.89 | 1 | 8 |
| PA de Silva | 35 | 32 | 3 | 1064 | 145 | 36.68 | 86.57 | 2 | 6 |
| IVA Richards | 23 | 21 | 5 | 1013 | 181 | 63.31 | 85.05 | 3 | 5 |
| ME Waugh | 22 | 22 | 3 | 1004 | 130 | 52.84 | 83.04 | 4 | 4 |
| RT Ponting | 28 | 27 | 3 | 998 | 140* | 41.58 | 74.98 | 3 | 2 |
| SR Waugh | 33 | 30 | 10 | 978 | 120* | 48.90 | 81.02 | 1 | 6 |
| A Ranatunga | 30 | 29 | 8 | 969 | 88* | 46.14 | 80.95 | - | 7 |
| BC Lara | 25 | 25 | 3 | 956 | 116 | 43.45 | 87.70 | 2 | 6 |
| Saeed Anwar | 21 | 21 | 4 | 915 | 113* | 53.82 | 79.08 | 3 | 3 |

## TEAM TOTALS

### Highest team totals:

| | | |
|---|---|---|
| 398-5 (50 overs) | Sri Lanka v. Kenya | Kandy, 1996 |
| 373-6 (50 overs) | India v. Sri Lanka | Taunton, 1999 |
| 360-4 (50 overs) | West Indies v. Sri Lanka | Karachi, 1987 |
| 359-2 (50 overs) | Australia v. India | Johannesburg, 2003 |
| 340-2 (50 overs) | Zimbabwe v. Namibia | Harare, 2003 |
| 338-5 (60 overs) | Pakistan v. Sri Lanka | Swansea, 1983 |
| 334-4 (60 overs) | England v. India | Lord's, 1975 |
| 333-9 (60 overs) | England v. Sri Lanka | Taunton, 1983 |
| 330-6 (60 overs) | Pakistan v. Sri Lanka | Nottingham, 1975 |
| 329-2 (50 overs) | India v. Kenya | Bristol, 1999 |

### Lowest team totals:

| | | |
|---|---|---|
| 36 (18.4 overs) | Canada v. Sri Lanka | Paarl, 2003 |
| 45 (14 overs) | Namibia v. Australia | Potchefstroom, 2003 |
| 45 (40.3 overs) | Canada v. England | Manchester, 1979 |
| 68 (31.3 overs) | Scotland v. West Indies | Leicester, 1999 |
| 74 (40.2 overs) | Pakistan v. England | Adelaide, 1991 |
| 84 (17.4 overs) | Namibia v. Pakistan | Kimberley, 2003 |
| 86 (37.2 overs) | Sri Lanka v. West Indies | Manchester, 1975 |
| 93 (35.2 overs) | West Indies v. Kenya | Pune, 1996 |
| 93 (36.2 overs) | England v. Australia | Leeds, 1975 |
| 94 (52.3 overs) | East Africa v. England | Birmingham, 1975 |

## FASTEST HUNDREDS

| Balls | 4s | 6s | Player | Match/Venue/Year |
|---|---|---|---|---|
| 67 | 7 | 6 | JM Davison | Canada v. West Indies, Centurion, 2003 |
| 72 | 16 | 6 | Kapil Dev | India v. Zimbabwe, Tunbridge Wells, 1983 |
| 82 | 12 | 2 | CH Lloyd | West Indies v. Australia, Lord's, 1975 |
| 83 | 16 | 0 | BC Lara | West Indies v. South Africa, Karachi, 1996 |
| 84 | 16 | 2 | SR Tendulkar | India v. Kenya, Bristol, 1999 |
| 85 | 10 | 3 | SM Gavaskar | India v. New Zealand, Nagpur, 1987 |

## BEST BOWLING FIGURES

| | | |
|---|---|---|
| 7-15 | GD McGrath | Australia v. Namibia, Potchefstroom, 2003 |
| 7-20 | AJ Bichel | Australia v. England, Port Elizabeth, 2003 |
| 7-51 | WW Davis | West Indies v. Australia, Leeds, 1983 |
| 6-14 | GJ Gilmour | Australia v. England, Leeds, 1975 |
| 6-23 | SE Bond | New Zealand v. Australia, Port Elizabeth, 2003 |
| 6-23 | A Nehra | India v. England, Durban, 2003 |
| 6-25 | WPUJC Vaas | Sri Lanka v. Bangladesh, Pietermaritzburg, 2003 |
| 6-39 | KH MacLeay | Australia v. India, Nottingham, 1983 |
| 5-14 | GD McGrath | Australia v. West Indies, Manchester, 1999 |
| 5-21 | L Klusener | South Africa v. Kenya, Amstelveen, 1999 |

## RECORD PARTNERSHIPS

| Wkt | Runs | Batsmen | Match/Venue/Year |
|-----|------|---------|------------------|
| 1st | 194 | Wajahatullah Wasti & Saeed Anwar | Pakistan v. New Zealand, Manchester, 1999 |
| 2nd | 318 | RS Dravid & SC Ganguly | India v. Sri Lanka, Taunton, 1999 |
| 3rd | 237* | RS Dravid & SR Tendulkar | India v. Kenya, Bristol, 1999 |
| 4th | 168 | LK Germon & CZ Harris | New Zealand v. Australia, Chennai, 1996 |
| 5th | 148 | CL Cairns & RG Twose | New Zealand v. Australia, Cardiff, 1999 |
| 6th | 161 | MO Odumbe & AV Vadher | Kenya v. Sri Lanka, Southampton, 1999 |
| 7th | 98 | RR Sarwan & RD Jacobs | West Indies v. New Zealand, Port Elizabeth, 2003 |
| 8th | 117 | DL Houghton & IP Butchart | Zimbabwe v. New Zealand, Hyderabad, 1987 |
| 9th | 126* | N Kapil Dev & SMH Kirmani | India v. Zimbabwe, Tunbridge Wells, 1983 |
| 10th | 71 | J Garner & AME Roberts | West Indies v. India, Manchester, 1983 |

**Building a platform:** The largest opening partnership in World Cup history was between Saeed Anwar (left) and Wajahatullah Wasti in 1999.

## MOST WICKETS

| Name | Mat | O | M | R | W | Ave | Best | 4w | 5w | SR |
|------|-----|---|---|---|---|-----|------|----|----|----|
| Wasim Akram | 38 | 324.3 | 17 | 1311 | 55 | 23.83 | 5–28 | 2 | 1 | 35.4 |
| GD McGrath | 28 | 245 | 37 | 935 | 45 | 20.77 | 7–15 | – | 2 | 32.6 |
| J Srinath | 34 | 283.2 | 21 | 1224 | 44 | 27.81 | 4–30 | 2 | – | 38.6 |
| AA Donald | 25 | 218.5 | 14 | 913 | 38 | 24.02 | 4–17 | 2 | – | 34.5 |
| WPUJC Vaas | 21 | 184 | 24 | 754 | 36 | 20.94 | 6–25 | 1 | 1 | 30.6 |
| Imran Khan | 28 | 169.3 | 18 | 655 | 34 | 19.26 | 4–37 | 2 | – | 29.9 |
| SK Warne | 17 | 162.5 | 16 | 624 | 32 | 19.50 | 4–29 | 4 | – | 30.5 |
| CZ Harris | 28 | 194.2 | 10 | 861 | 32 | 26.90 | 4–7 | 1 | – | 36.4 |
| M Muralitharan | 21 | 187.5 | 13 | 693 | 30 | 23.10 | 4–28 | 1 | – | 37.5 |
| IT Botham | 22 | 222 | 33 | 762 | 30 | 25.40 | 4–31 | 1 | – | 44.4 |

## MOST CATCHES

- **18** RT Ponting (Australia)
- **16** CL Cairns (New Zealand)
- **15** ST Jayasuriya (Sri Lanka)
- **14** PA de Silva (Sri Lanka)
- **14** A Kumble (India)
- **14** SR Waugh (Australia)
- **13** CL Hooper (West Indies)
- **12** DL Haynes (West Indies)
- **12** GA Hick (England)
- **12** Inzamam-ul-Haq (Pakistan)
- **12** Kapil Dev (India)
- **12** CH Lloyd (West Indies)

## MOST MATCHES

| Name | Mat | Runs | Ave | W | Ave | Ct | St |
|------|-----|------|-----|---|-----|----|----|
| Wasim Akram | 38 | 426 | 19.36 | 55 | 23.83 | 8 | - |
| PA de Silva | 35 | 1064 | 36.68 | 16 | 41.93 | 14 | - |
| J Srinath | 34 | 85 | 9.44 | 44 | 27.81 | 4 | - |
| SR Tendulkar | 33 | 1732 | 59.72 | 6 | 78.16 | 10 | - |
| Javed Miandad | 33 | 1083 | 43.32 | 4 | 18.25 | 10 | 1 |
| SR Waugh | 33 | 978 | 48.90 | 27 | 30.14 | 14 | - |
| Inzamam-ul-Haq | 32 | 643 | 23.81 | - | - | 12 | - |
| A Ranatunga | 30 | 969 | 46.14 | 6 | 76.66 | 7 | - |
| M Azharuddin | 30 | 826 | 39.33 | 5 | 21.80 | 11 | - |
| A Flower | 30 | 815 | 32.60 | - | - | 12 | 3 |

## OLDEST PLAYERS

| | | |
|---|---|---|
| 47y 257d | NE Clarke | Netherlands v. South Africa, Rawalpindi, 1996 |
| 44y 306d | AJ Traicos | Zimbabwe v. England, Albury, 1992 |
| 43y 236d | JL Louw | Namibia v. Zimbabwe, Harare, 2003 |
| 43y 129d | GJAF Aponso | Netherlands v. South Africa, Rawalpindi, 1996 |
| 43y 44d | DJ Pringle | East Africa v. England, Birmingham, 1975 |
| 42y 347d | SW Lubbers | Netherlands v. South Africa, Rawalpindi, 1996 |
| 41y 9d | DS de Silva | Sri Lanka v. England, Leeds, 1983 |
| 40y 349d | IL Philip | Scotland v. Bangladesh, Edinburgh, 1999 |
| 40y 251d | LR Gibbs | West Indies v. Sri Lanka, Manchester, 1975 |
| 40y 39d | O Henry | South Africa v. Sri Lanka, Wellington, 1992 |

**Sachin Tendulkar:** One of the legends of cricket, the Indian master has scored more runs in the tournament than any other player.

## YOUNGEST PLAYERS

| | | |
|---|---|---|
| 17y 70d | T Jubair | Bangladesh v. West Indies, Benoni, 2003 |
| 17y 237d | SP Pasqual | Sri Lanka v. New Zealand, Nottingham, 1979 |
| 17y 282d | TM Odoyo | Kenya v. India, Cuttack, 1996 |
| 17y 364d | J Miandad | Pakistan v. West Indies, Birmingham, 1975 |
| 18y 115d | Z Fazal | Pakistan v. India, Sydney, 1992 |
| 18y 222d | M Ashraful | Bangladesh v. Sri Lanka, Pietermaritzburg, 2003 |
| 18y 237d | AN Ranasinghe | Sri Lanka v. West Indies, Manchester, 1975 |
| 18y 262d | M Sheikh | Kenya v. England, Canterbury, 1999 |
| 18y 304d | SR Tendulkar | India v. England, Perth, 1992 |
| 18y 351d | B Zuiderent | Netherlands v. New Zealand, Vadodara, 1996 |

# TEA INTERVAL: CRICKET WORLD CUP QUIZ

If you've taken in all the information within these pages, then the following quiz should be a doddle. It's time to test your knowledge of the greatest cricket tournament in the world. (Answers on page 80.)

1. Name the player who has played in the most Cricket World Cup matches.
2. Against which team did Sri Lanka hammer a Cricket World Cup record total of 398 for 5 in 1996?
3. Name the five sides to have won the Cricket World Cup.
4. Who holds the record for the fastest Cricket World Cup century?
5. Who is the leading run-scorer in the history of the Cricket World Cup?
6. The two debutants aside, which other 2007 World Cup qualifier has yet to record a Cricket World Cup win?
7. Who is the oldest player to have played in the Cricket World Cup?
8. Which team have won the most Cricket World Cup matches?
9. Who is the only captain to have lifted the Cricket World Cup twice?
10. Which team have been Cricket World Cup runners-up the most times?
11. Who holds the record for Cricket World Cup's highest individual score?
12. Which two teams will be making their Cricket World Cup debuts in 2007?
13. Who is the leading wicket-taker in Cricket World Cup history?
14. Who has held on to the most catches in the Cricket World Cup?
15. Who has recorded the best bowling analysis in a Cricket World Cup match?
16. Which team did Sri Lanka bowl out for 36, the Cricket World Cup's lowest total, in 2003?
17. Which two players hit a Cricket World Cup record partnership of 318 against Sri Lanka in 1999?
18. Who is the youngest player to have played in the Cricket World Cup?
19. Name Sri Lanka's 1987 and 1999 Cricket World Cup-winning coach.
20. Which team has appeared in the most Cricket World Cup finals?

## PICTURE QUIZ

A. **Reasons to be cheerful** …

Name the year and the players featured in these celebratory photos.

B. **Who are ya?**

Name the players in this mysterious sextet.

C. **Tattooed heroes**

Name the proud owners of these decorated biceps (and forearms).

# A. REASONS TO BE CHEERFUL...

1

2

3

# B. WHO ARE YA?

1

2

3

4

5

6

# C. TATTOOED HEROES

1

2

3

## GROUP A (all matches played at Warner Park, Basseterre, St Kitts)

| | Toss (bat/field) | 1st innings | 2nd innings | Result |
|---|---|---|---|---|
| Wed 14 March<br>Australia v. Scotland | ................ | ................ | ................ | Ausbtscot |
| Fri 16 March<br>Netherlands v. South Africa | ............ | ................ | ................ | SAbtNed |
| Sun 18 March<br>Australia v. Netherlands | ................ | ................ | ................ | AusbtNed |
| Tue 20 March<br>Scotland v. South Africa | ................ | ................ | ................ | SAbtSt |
| Thu 22 March<br>Netherlands v. Scotland | ................ | ................ | ................ | |
| Sat 24 March<br>Australia v. South Africa | ................ | ................ | ................ | AusbtSa |

### Final Group A Table

| | P | W | L | NR | Pts | NetRR |
|---|---|---|---|---|---|---|
| A1. Australia | | | | | 6 | |
| A2. South Africa | | | | | 4 | |
| A3. | | | | | 2 | |
| A4. | | | | | 0 | |

## GROUP B (all matches played at Queen's Park Oval, Port of Spain, Trinidad)

| | Toss (bat/field) | 1st innings | 2nd innings | Result |
|---|---|---|---|---|
| Thu 15 March<br>Bermuda v. Sri Lanka | ................ | ................ | ................ | SLbtBer |
| Sat 17 March<br>Bangladesh v. India | ................ | ................ | ................ | BanbteInc |
| Mon 19 March<br>Bermuda v. India | ................ | ................ | ................ | |
| Wed 21 March<br>Bangladesh v. Sri Lanka | ................ | ................ | ................ | SLbtBan |
| Fri 23 March<br>India v. Sri Lanka | ................ | ................ | ................ | SLbtInd |
| Sun 25 March<br>Bangladesh v. Bermuda | ................ | ................ | ................ | BanbtBer |

### Final Group B Table

| | P | W | L | NR | Pts | NetRR |
|---|---|---|---|---|---|---|
| B1. Sri Lanka | | | | | | |
| B2. Bangladesh | | | | | | |
| B3. | | | | | | |
| B4. | | | | | | |

## GROUP C (all matches played at Beausejour Stadium, Gros Islet, St Lucia)

| | Toss (bat/field) | 1st innings | 2nd innings | Result |
|---|---|---|---|---|
| Wed 14 March<br>Canada v. Kenya | ................ | ................ | ................ | |
| Fri 16 March<br>England v. New Zealand | ................ | ................ | ................ | NZbtEng |
| Sun 18 March<br>Canada v. England | ................ | ................ | ................ | Engbtcan |
| Tue 20 March<br>Kenya v. New Zealand | ................ | ................ | ................ | NZbtken |
| Thu 22 March<br>Canada v. New Zealand | ................ | ................ | ................ | NZbtcan |
| Sat 24 March<br>England v. Kenya | ................ | ................ | ................ | Engbtken |

### Final Group D Table

| | P | W | L | NR | Pts | NetRR |
|---|---|---|---|---|---|---|
| C1. New Zealand | | | | | 6 | |
| C2. England | | | | | 4 | |
| C3. | | | | | 2 | |
| C4. | | | | | 0 | |

## GROUP D (all matches played at Sabina Park, Kingston, Jamaica)

| | Toss (bat/field) | 1st innings | 2nd innings | Result |
|---|---|---|---|---|
| Tue 13 March<br>West Indies v. Pakistan | ................ | ................ | ................ | WIbtpak |
| Thu 15 March<br>Ireland v. Zimbabwe | ................ | ................ | ................ | Irebtzim |
| Sat 17 March<br>Ireland v. Pakistan | ................ | ................ | ................ | Irebtpak |
| Mon 19 March<br>West Indies v. Zimbabwe | ................ | ................ | ................ | WIbtzim |
| Wed 21 March<br>Pakistan v. Zimbabwe | ................ | ................ | ................ | |
| Fri 23 March<br>Ireland v. West Indies | ................ | ................ | ................ | WIbtIre |

### Final Group D Table

| | P | W | L | NR | Pts | NetRR |
|---|---|---|---|---|---|---|
| D1. WI | | | | | 6 | |
| D2. Ireland | | | | | 4 | |
| D3. | | | | | 2 | |
| D4. | | | | | 0 | |

## SUPER EIGHTS

| | Toss (bat/field) | 1st innings | 2nd innings | Result |
|---|---|---|---|---|
| **Tue 27 March**, Sir Vivian Richards Stadium, Antigua | | | | |
| D2 v. A1 | .................. | .................. | .................. | ........... |
| **Wed 28 March**, Providence Stadium, Guyana | | | | |
| A2 v. B1 | .................. | .................. | .................. | ........... |
| **Thu 29 March**, Sir Vivian Richards Stadium, Antigua | | | | |
| D2 v. C1 | .................. | .................. | .................. | ........... |
| **Fri 30 March**, Providence Stadium, Guyana | | | | |
| D1 v. C2 | .................. | .................. | .................. | ........... |
| **Sat 31 March**, Sir Vivian Richards Stadium, Antigua | | | | |
| A1 v. B2 | .................. | .................. | .................. | ........... |
| **Sun 1 April**, Providence Stadium, Guyana | | | | |
| D2 v. B1 | .................. | .................. | .................. | ........... |
| **Mon 2 April**, Sir Vivian Richards Stadium, Antigua | | | | |
| B2 v. C1 | .................. | .................. | .................. | ........... |
| **Tue 3 April**, Providence Stadium, Guyana | | | | |
| D1 v. A2 | .................. | .................. | .................. | ........... |
| **Wed 4 April**, Sir Vivian Richards Stadium, Antigua | | | | |
| C2 v. B1 | .................. | .................. | .................. | ........... |
| **Sat 7 April**, Providence Stadium, Guyana | | | | |
| B2 v. A2 | .................. | .................. | .................. | ........... |
| **Sun 8 April**, Sir Vivian Richards Stadium, Antigua | | | | |
| A1 v. C2 | .................. | .................. | .................. | ........... |
| **Mon 9 April**, Providence Stadium, Guyana | | | | |
| D1 v. C1 | .................. | .................. | .................. | ........... |
| **Tue 10 April**, National Cricket Stadium, St George's, Grenada | | | | |
| D2 v. A2 | .................. | .................. | .................. | ........... |
| **Wed 11 April**, Kensington Oval, Bridgetown, Barbados | | | | |
| C2 v. B2 | .................. | .................. | .................. | ........... |
| **Thu 12 April**, National Cricket Stadium, St George's, Grenada | | | | |
| B1 v. C1 | .................. | .................. | .................. | ........... |
| **Fri 13 April**, Kensington Oval, Bridgetown, Barbados | | | | |
| A1 v. D1 | .................. | .................. | .................. | ........... |
| **Sat 14 April**, National Cricket Stadium, St George's, Grenada | | | | |
| A2 v. C1 | .................. | .................. | .................. | ........... |
| **Sun 15 April**, Kensington Oval, Bridgetown, Barbados | | | | |
| B2 v. D1 | .................. | .................. | .................. | ........... |
| **Mon 16 April**, National Cricket Stadium, St George's, Grenada | | | | |
| A1 v. B1 | .................. | .................. | .................. | ........... |
| **Tue 17 April**, Kensington Oval, Bridgetown, Barbados | | | | |
| A2 v. C2 | .................. | .................. | .................. | ........... |
| **Wed 18 April**, National Cricket Stadium, St George's, Grenada | | | | |
| D1 v. B1 | .................. | .................. | .................. | ........... |
| **Thu 19 April**, Kensington Oval, Bridgetown, Barbados | | | | |
| D2 v. B2 | .................. | .................. | .................. | ........... |
| **Fri 20 April**, National Cricket Stadium, St George's, Grenada | | | | |
| A1 v. C1 | .................. | .................. | .................. | ........... |
| **Sat 21 April**, Kensington Oval, Bridgetown, Barbados | | | | |
| D2 v. C2 | .................. | .................. | .................. | ........... |

## FINAL SUPER EIGHTS TABLE

| | | P | W | L | NR | Pts | NetRR |
|---|---|---|---|---|---|---|---|
| 1. | .................... | ........ | ........ | ........ | ........ | ........ | ........ |
| 2. | .................... | ........ | ........ | ........ | ........ | ........ | ........ |
| 3. | .................... | ........ | ........ | ........ | ........ | ........ | ........ |
| 4. | .................... | ........ | ........ | ........ | ........ | ........ | ........ |
| 5. | .................... | ........ | ........ | ........ | ........ | ........ | ........ |
| 6. | .................... | ........ | ........ | ........ | ........ | ........ | ........ |
| 7. | .................... | ........ | ........ | ........ | ........ | ........ | ........ |
| 8. | .................... | ........ | ........ | ........ | ........ | ........ | ........ |

Note: Points against any group stage opponents carried through.

## SEMI-FINALS

| | Toss (bat/field) | 1st innings | 2nd innings | Result |
|---|---|---|---|---|
| **Tue 24 April**, Sabina Park, Kingston, Jamaica | | | | |
| 1st Semi-final – 2 v. 3 | .................. | .................. | .................. | ........... |
| **Wed 25 April**, Beausejour Stadium, Gros Islet, St Lucia | | | | |
| 2nd Semi-final – 1 v. 4 | .................. | .................. | .................. | ........... |

## WORLD CUP FINAL 2007
### Saturday 28 April, Kensington Oval, Bridgetown, Barbados

....................................................... v. ...........................................

**FIRST INNINGS**

...........................................
...........................................
...........................................
...........................................
...........................................
...........................................
...........................................
...........................................
...........................................
...........................................

b ....... lb ....... nb ....... w ......

TOTAL        for ..... wickets ........

FoW 1 .... 2 .... 3 .... 4 .... 5 .... 6 .... 7 .... 8 .... 9 .... 10 ....

BOWLING    O  M  R  W  nb  w
...........................................
...........................................
...........................................
...........................................
...........................................
...........................................

**SECOND INNINGS**

...........................................
...........................................
...........................................
...........................................
...........................................
...........................................
...........................................
...........................................
...........................................
...........................................

b ....... lb ....... nb ....... w ......

TOTAL        for ..... wickets ........

FoW 1 .... 2 .... 3 .... 4 .... 5 .... 6 .... 7 .... 8 .... 9 .... 10 ....

O  M  R  W  nb  w
...........................................
...........................................
...........................................
...........................................
...........................................
...........................................

## WORLD CUP CHAMPIONS 2007

.......................................................................................................

# PICTURE ACKNOWLEDGEMENTS

The publishers would like to thank the following sources for their kind permission to reproduce the pictures in this book.

**Action Images:** /Andy Clark/Reuters: 43; /John Sibley: 24

**Carlton Books Ltd:** /Karl Adamson: 64tl, 64ctl, 64cbl, 64bl, 64cr, 64br

**Cricket Europe:** /Barry Chambers: 27, 34bl, 35; /Joe Curtis: 16; /Alec Davies: 51tr

**Corbis Images:** /David Cumming/Eye Ubiquitous: 59tr; /Richard Cummins: 65; /Stephen Frink/Zefa: 52br; /Catherine Karnow: 52tr; /Layne Kennedy: 63; /Bob Krist: 52c, 58, 59b; /Robert Harding World Imagery: 52tl

**Empics:** /AP: 20t; Gemunu Amarasinghe/AP: 77cbc; /Sayyid Azim/AP: 41; /Shirley Bahadur/AP: 4-5; Benedict/AP: 12; /Chris Brandis/AP: 62; /Ben Curtis/PA: 29l; /David Davies/PA: 44tr; /Adam Davy: 37l, 44bl; /Sean Dempsey: 33bl; /Paul Ellis/AP: 38l, /Paul Faith/PA: 50; /Nigel French: 21; /Themba Hadebe/AP: 48; /Noel Hammond: 71br; /Tom Hevezi/PA: 22bl; /Steve Holland/AP: 28; /Hrusa/AP: 2tr; /David Jones/PA: 77cbl; /M. Lakshman/AP: 77ctr; /Andres Leighton/AP: 46l; /Tony Marshall: 23, 25, 75bl; /Toby Melville/PA: 71tl; /Steve Mitchell: 42tr; /Rebecca Naden/PA: 34tr, 39, 47, 77ctc, 77bl; /PA: 51bl, 56, 68; /Rick Rycroft/AP: 18-19; /S&G: 54, 55, 57bl, 66-67; /Aman Sharma/AP: 30bl, 30tr, 31; /Neal Simpson: 29r, 36, 57bc, 77tr; /Michael Steele: 72-73; /Rui Vieira/PA: 77cbr, 77ctl; /John Walton: 32; /Chris Young/PA: 38r

**Getty Images:** 2br, 6;  /Slim Aarons: 60; /Alessandro Abbonizio/AFP: 33tr; /Hamish Blair: 13, 20b, 37r, 49; /Shaun Botterill: 42bl; /Peter Cade/Stone: 64tr; /Emmaunuel Dunand/AFP: 1, 2tl, 10-11; /Laurence Griffiths: 57tr, 75tr; /Clive Mason: 2c, 40bl; /Michael Melford/National Geographic: 61; /Adrian Murrell: 2bl, 69, 77tl; /Aamir Qureshi/AFP: 45; /Ben Radford: 26bl, 70, 77tc; /Haider Shah/AFP: 26tr; /Tom Shaw: 77bc; /Michael Thomas: 46r; /Touchline Photo: 40tr; /Kevin West: 52bl; /Duif du Toit/Touchline: 22tr

**Photos 12:** /Collection Cinema: 77br

Every effort has been made to acknowledge correctly and contact the source and/or copyright holder of each picture and Carlton Books Limited apologises for any unintentional errors or omissions, which will be, corrected in future editions of this book.

**Answers from page 76**

1 Wasim Akram (38). 2 Kenya. 3 West Indies, India, Australia, Pakistan and Sri Lanka.
4 John Davison (Canada v. West Indies, 2003). 5 Sachin Tendulkar (1,732 runs). 6 Scotland.
7 Nolan Clarke (Netherlands v. South Africa, 1996). 8 Australia (40). 9 Clive Lloyd.
10 England (3). 11 Gary Kirsten (188 not out, South Africa v. UAE, 1996). 12 Bermuda and Ireland. 13 Wasim Akram (55). 14 Ricky Ponting (18). 15 Glenn McGrath (7 for 15, Australia v. Namibia, 2003). 16 Canada. 17 Rahul Dravid and Sachin Tendulkar. 18 Talha Jubair (Bangladesh v. West Indies, 2003). 19 Tom Moody. 20 Australia.

## PICTURE QUIZ

### A. Reasons to be cheerful

1 1983. India: Kapil Dev (left) and Mohinder Armanath. 2 1992. (Pakistan, left to right): Mahmood Fazil, Wasim Akram and Aamir Sohail. 3 1999. (Australia, left to right): Steve Waugh, Shane Warne and Mark Waugh.

### B. Who are ya?

1 Ricky Ponting (Australia). 2 Dwayne Bravo (West Indies). 3 Rahul Dravid (India). 4 Abdul Razzaq (Pakistan). 5 Muttiah Muralitharan (Sri Lanka). 6 Shaun Pollock (South Africa).

### C. Tattooed heroes

1 Andrew Flintoff. 2 Kevin Pietersen. 3 Popeye the Sailorman. (OK. We're fairly sure our muscular seafaring friend never actually played cricket, but Abdul Razzaq of Pakistan gulped down pounds of spinach on a recent tour of Australia to be nicknamed "Popeye" and, judging by his recent hitting exploits, the spinach seems to work for him too!)